375.001
C93

117357

DATE DUE			
Sep 27 '81			
Oct 19 de			
Nov 16 '81			
Dec 11 '81			
'82			
Mar 1			
Mar 29 '82			
Apr 30 '82			
R. -UNCG			
Poman.			
Dec 10 '82			

WITHDRAWN

CURRICULUM CHANGE
TOWARD THE 21st CENTURY

By Harold G. Shane

The Curriculum Series

CARL A. RUDISILL LIBRARY
LENOIR RHYNE COLLEGE

National Education Association
Washington, D.C.

Copyright © 1977
National Education Association of the United States

Stock No. 1708-0-00 (paper)

Library of Congress Cataloging in Publication Data

Curriculum change toward the 21st century.

(The Curriculum series)
Bibliography: p.
1. Curriculum change—Addresses, essays, lectures.
I. Shane, Harold Gray, 1914-   II. National Educa-
tion Association. III. Series.
LB1570.C8839   375'.001   77-2551
ISBN 0-8106-2104-5
ISBN 0-8106-2103-7 pbk.

375.001
C93
117357
march 1981

Note

The opinions expressed in this publication should not be construed as representing
the policy or position of the National Education Association. Materials published as
part of the NEA Professional Studies Series are intended to be discussion documents for teachers who are concerned with specialized interests of the profession.

Dr. Harold G. Shane is University Professor of Education at Indiana University, Bloomington. A noted author and editor of
books on contemporary education, Dr. Shane is also a Past
President of the Association for Supervision and Curriculum
Development.

CONTENTS

FOREWORD

In 1972, the National Education Association established a Bicentennial Committee charged with developing a "living commemoration of the principles of the American Revolution." This 200th anniversary celebration of the Declaration of Independence was to focus on the *next* 100 years of education in an interdependent global community.

The initial work of the committee culminated in the NEA *Bicentennial Ideabook.* Among the ideas it contained was the development of a definitive volume to "contain a reframing of the cardinal principles of education and recommendations for a global curriculum." After recognizing the importance of the original cardinal principles, which were published in 1918, the committee made the point that "today, most policy statements about education are obsolete; education, taken as a whole, is not adequate to the times and too seldom anticipates the future."

The present report, *Curriculum Change Toward the 21st Century,* proposes cardinal premises to guide curriculum development that anticipates the 21st century. It also is a direct and immediate outgrowth of the Bicentennial Committee's belief that "educators around the world are in a unique position to bring about a harmoniously interdependent global community based on the principles of peace and justice."

Early in September 1975, a 22-member Pre-Planning Committee—including four NEA staff members—began the task of recasting the seven cardinal principles of education. While committee members did not reach a consensus on every point, they did generally agree that distinguished world citizens, competent educators, and youth should be interviewed, either on tape or in person, and their views incorporated into the report; that heed should be given to the geographic divisions and ethnic fabric of both American and world culture; that conservative as well as liberal opinions from persons in a variety of disciplines should be gathered; and that panel members' images of the future should be obtained along with the educational changes that these views suggested.

In addition, the planning group also noted that any reports resulting from the re-examination of the cardinal principles, however useful they might be, would *not* automatically become NEA policy statements since such statements are an Association function. It also was clearly recognized that the project was not to masquerade as *research* but to be presented as informed *opinion* which, in some instances, was familiar with research.

During the planning period, the Pre-Planning Committee nominated nearly 250 persons for the 30 or more interviews that originally were planned. The committee screened these nominees to reduce the international panel to a more manageable size. This smaller list was then studied individually by committee members, most of whom sent in a ballot indicating the names of the 15 persons whose views they believed would be most reliable, interesting, and influential. Using a list based on these stated preferences, the project staff and representatives of the NEA selected the persons to be interviewed.

When approached, most of the nominees were pleased to participate in the interviews. Beginning in mid-September, a total of 46 panel members and approximately 95 youth—most of them in their junior or senior years of secondary school—summarized their views on tapes that ran for more than 80 hours. The panel members responded to three questions:[1]

1. In broad terms, and barring such catastrophes as nuclear war, what are some of the characteristics of the most probable world you foresee by the 21st century?
2. In view of this image of the future, what imperative skills should education seek to develop? Also, in anticipation of the 21st century world, what premises should guide educational planning?
3. Have the original seven cardinal principles of education retained their merit? If so, what are the new ways in which they should now be interpreted, amended, or applied in anticipation of the changing social, economic, and political conditions in the world community?

Persons responding to these questions invariably spoke at length, and interviews ran from 25 minutes to almost two hours.

---

[1]The students responded to the following questions: What do you think the world will be like 20 years from now? What would you *like* to be doing 20 years from now, and what do you think you *will* be doing in 1995? What do you think education could do to help you reach your personal life goals? Are these goals [the seven cardinal principles] still good ones after nearly 60 years?

CHAPTER I
INTRODUCTION

THE HUMAN OPPORTUNITY. Historians writing a century hence in 2076 may well describe the interval between 1976 and 2001 as one of the most portentous in the human story. As these years unwind, there is an opportunity for humankind to approach both its age-old dreams and true greatness as it draws near the threshold of a millennium in which it is to be hoped that devastating and relatively cheap weapon systems are controlled, tensions between selfish desire and the common good are brought into balance, conflicts among social groups are reduced, and the deeper meanings of life are more fully probed and understood.

The human race, we must remember, already has come an enormous distance in the 20th century. Today, no U.S. president or leaders in other nations would boast of imperialistic ventures or disregard the human rights of the peoples in less developed nations. Moral and political pressures have begun to reduce the abuses of big business, big government, and big labor. The machinations and illegal operations of government agencies are under sharp scrutiny. Political knavery seems at low ebb after the trauma of the Watergate scandals. Steps are being taken to keep the world's waterways from becoming open sewers. The welfare of large numbers of humans has been served by legislation for the poor, the disadvantaged, and the handicapped. Other examples of progress toward a sane and humane world community exist in abundance.

But humanity has also had a long list of problems with which to cope—a list that could grow longer before it grows shorter. Consider the situation in the United States during the past 10 or 15 years! President John F. Kennedy, Martin Luther King and Robert Kennedy were gunned down, drug abuse increased sharply, and the crime rate climbed. For a variety of reasons—the struggle in Southeast Asia among them—America's overseas image became tarnished while the influence of her leadership plummeted. To add to the national malaise, large segments of Watts and of Washington, D.C., burned to smoking heaps of rubble during riots, university laboratories were bombed or otherwise damaged, a substantial minority of youth expressed its alienation through what Theodore Roszak labeled a "counter culture," and some died at Kent State University. More recently, a president was drummed out of office, numerous abuses by corporations came to light, a labor leader—James Hoffa—disappeared and presumably was murdered, inflation reached alarming levels, unemployment was at its highest levels since the Great Depression of the 1930's, and Robert Heilbroner gloomily proclaimed after his inquiry into the human future that "we affluent Americans will have to give up a great deal."[1]

Nor did it help to have Barry Commoner warn that unchecked pollution would eventually destroy the planet's capacity to support human life[2] or to read historian Geoffrey Barraclough's depressing conclusion that many Americans felt shortages of raw materials and resources such as oil were likely to be chronic and that even modest levels of affluence might not be reached.[3]

PREVIEW OF A WORLD IN TRANSITION. At a time rife with uncertainties, a time of relativism and "permissiveness" when old values are being severely questioned and new ones have not yet clearly replaced them, the teaching profession in the United States—and indeed the world—has enormous opportunities and responsibilities. As Norman Cousins put it, "Since human nature is always changing, one of the purposes of education is to see that it changes for the better."[4]

This publication has been designed to present an overview of what Stuart Chase once called "the most probable world" as it may emerge in the next quarter century—a preview of a troubled yet exciting planetary transition—as conceived by the NEA Interna-

---

[1] Colin Campbell, "Coming Apart at the Seams: An Interview with Robert Heilbroner," *Psychology Today,* February 1975, p. 97.

[2] Quoted in *Saturday Review,* September 20, 1969, p. 56.

[3] Geoffrey Barraclough, "The Great World Crisis (I)," *The New York Review of Books,* January 23, 1975, p. 20.

[4] Unless otherwise noted, persons quoted in the text were members of NEA's International Panel and their statements are taken from interview tapes.

tional Panel during 1976. It is deeply concerned with the question of *how* education can improve human nature.

THE LIMITATIONS OF UTOPIA.   Readers will find that teachers and their schools in coming decades, as the NEA panelists saw them, will not be operating in the sort of moral, social, and political utopia that Thomas More described in 1516. In other words, there will continue to be limits to the kinds of ideal situations that one might wish for. Schools in some instances will continue to operate on limited budgets, in aging plants that may leave much to be desired, and to work with students some of whom will be obstinate, hyperactive, slow to learn, and so badly battered by life as to appear churlish or threatening. Yet there is a bright side to the picture.

A HUMAN NEEDS CURRICULUM.   Despite constraints such as those mentioned above, the 1980's and 1990's should present unprecedented opportunities to create a lifelong "human needs curriculum" to serve persons of all ages. As the testimony of the panelists' tapes bears witness, many thoughtful persons in many different walks of life believe that traditional and conventional boundaries of U.S. education must no longer confine teaching–learning processes. The tasks of finding new and different boundaries for education promises to enrich and cross-fertilize the many forms that schooling is likely to assume between 10 and 20 years hence. It is to these tasks that *Curriculum Change Toward the 21st Century* addresses itself.

WHAT THIS BOOK SEEKS TO ACCOMPLISH.   The objectives of *Curriculum Change Toward the 21st Century* can be summarized quickly. Chapter II presents the images of the future which the panelists seemed to share, along with some of their conflicting opinions. These views suggest the probable world in which education, including public and independent schooling, is likely to be operating. Chapter III offers speculations about human potential in an increasingly interdependent world community.

Chapter IV—a crucial section of the book—presents an updating and a reformulation of the NEA's seven cardinal principles that were originally published in 1918. In effect, this chapter presents extended and reaffirmed educational goals for the teaching profession to consider between 1976 and 2001.

Cardinal premises that are designed to guide educational practice for the next 25 years are presented in Chapter V. These premises, some 28 in all, suggest changes and reforms in instruction that teachers and parents may wish to consider as they strive to improve opportunities and identify responsibilities for the children, youth, and adults served by American education.

Unlike some education publications concerned with goals or new directions, *Curriculum Change Toward the 21st Century* seeks to face the challenge of moving from speculations and theory to the application of the 28 cardinal premises both within and beyond the walls of U.S. schools. To serve this purpose, Chapter VI concerns itself with the question of how parents, teachers, and other members of the adult community best can work together in determining educational needs in local districts, and how children and youth, too, can be involved. In short, Chapter VI focuses on *process*—on how people can work together to bring about a reformation or "quiet revolution" in teaching so that Americans of many ages and backgrounds are equipped with the skills and knowledge that the years ahead seem likely to demand.

Chapter VII, drawing on the 28 cardinal premises, discusses some changes for schooling in the United States. First, changes and trends bearing on education are inventoried and examined. Next, ten criteria for judging instruction are inferred from the 28 cardinal premises. Finally, a timetable for educational change is proposed.

In Chapter VIII, attention is directed to the matter of how content may change if certain of the cardinal premises are applied to curriculum development. The unique nature of individual schools is stressed as is the need to personalize education for learners and to develop positive, socially desirable attitudes. Without specifically prescribing content, nine areas of knowledge are identified and considerable attention is given to the question of how school curriculum and administrative organization could change if the 28 premises are used as guidelines. The chapter ends with a close look at teaching and learning that are not bound by classroom walls.

The concluding section, Chapter IX, directs attention to the total school as a center for personalized learning. Here the instructional program is examined in relation to (1) the community, (2) basic academic instruction, (3) avenues for experience that can be opened to children and youth, (4) "service and action learning," and (5) moral education and the development of ethical character.

Over 300 direct quotations from the panelists are presented in the Appendix. These excerpts, taken from approximately 80 hours of tape, are of interest as an expression of international viewpoints on education as of 1976. The statements also provide new meanings for the seven cardinal principles and documentation for the 28 cardinal premises assembled in Chapter V.

While it must be recognized that the responses of the panelists were many and varied, the writer has endeavored to present faithfully the spectrum of opinion which the NEA Project sought to obtain in its quest for guidelines that would provide a wholesome, humane, and intellectually strong education—a lifelong sequence of continuous opportunities for learning from early childhood to senior, past-60 learners.

CHAPTER II
IMAGES OF THE NEXT 25 YEARS

IMAGES OF 2001 ARE IMPORTANT. A cursory glance at today's newspaper headlines or five minutes spent listening to a wrap-up on the evening TV newscasts should suffice to prove that people everywhere are subjected to the pressures of technological, social, and economic change. In an era in which the old order of things in the industrial world and in its social system is showing structural defects and where many possible new developments are still in the blueprint stage, our images of educational futures become of consummate importance.

As Alvin Toffler[1] pointed out, in the first chapter of *Learning for Tomorrow,* "All education springs from some image of the future," and, indeed, so do most human activities. If we lack a clear vision of the future we seek, we lack both goals and the guidelines that help us to reach them. Furthermore, what we believe tomorrow will bring is likely to foreshadow our actual future simply because we hold these beliefs. There is yet another exceedingly crucial point to keep in mind. When we make judgments or predictions about a probable world of the future, we are voicing a call to *action* whether we realize it or not. That is, forecasts tend to initiate processes that will reduce possible problems that are foreseen, and they tend to suggest how we best can adapt to our assumptions about changing conditions.

As self-fulfilling prophecies, our images are very likely to determine the realities of 1996 or 2001. Before we re-examine the seven cardinal principles and review educational needs and changes suggested by premises for improving instruction, let us look through the eyes of the NEA panel and glimpse some of their

---

[1]Alvin Toffler, ed., *Learning for Tomorrow.* New York: Random House, 1974. p. 3.

hopes for humankind as well as some of the problems, constraints, and opportunities they foresee in the troubled yet exciting times that lie ahead.

THE WORLD WE MAY INHABIT BY 2001. Without exception, the world citizens[2] who were asked to envision the future expressed the strong opinion that the entire planet is involved in a tremendous human revolution for which history has no previous parallel, except perhaps in the disruptive changes that followed the collapse of Roman power in the Mediterranean world during the third century.

The disconcerting changes that are taking place both in the industrially developed world and in less developed countries are indications of a great discontinuity—a massive rupture—in the growth and development of the industrial society which has dominated or influenced much of the earth's surface, especially during the first three-quarters of the present century.

One of the prominent characteristics of the present period of rapid transition is the increasing interdependence of our species. Persuasive rhetoric is unnecessary to make the point that *any* country's problems anywhere are now *every* country's problems everywhere. Interdependence on a global scale already is a reality, whether or not we are quite ready to accept it. The task thus becomes one of adapting to this new reality and to the need for what Barbara Ward has labeled "dynamic reciprocity" between nations as they become more and more aware of their mutual need for one another's goods and services.

As we adjust to the new tempos of an increasingly crowded planet, it becomes important to identify some of the developments that already are influencing the future in certain ways. This not only helps us to understand *now* what is shaping the probable life-styles of 20 or 25 years hence; it also should help us to begin the thinking and the planning needed as we seek to cope with emerging problems and to make the most of certain opportunities which, fortunately, such problems also bring with them. Panel members men-

---

[2]While the individual views of participants are faithfully presented, the panelists spoke with many voices and no participant is necessarily associated with the points made hereafter unless that person is directly quoted in the Appendix to this effect.

tioned a number of developments likely to affect the lives of persons in every country, whether affluent or poor, weak or powerful, industrialized or developing, resource-rich or resource-poor.[3] These were as follows:

1. Continued acceleration in the rate of change. Although not all members of the NEA panel saw exactly the same events taking place, they generally agreed that the hallmark of the next two or three decades would be a continued and perhaps an accelerating rate of social change. Underlying processes for change presumably would result from continued growth in capital investment, in human knowledge, and in technology. Also of importance in generating continued change are shifts in attitudes, in our perceptions of the world about us, and in increasing levels of aspirations both in the United States and overseas.[4]

2. Greater complexity. Regardless of whether we are pleased or alarmed by the impact of technology on the 20th century, we can expect the complexity of life to increase because of the technological breakthroughs that constantly occur. Furthermore, in an interdependent world laced together by a network of communication lines and by a web of international trade, efforts to satisfy mutual needs will inevitably cause intricate problems. Japan's oil supply illustrates both interdependence and the importance of a complex transport system in the world of 1976. Japan often has no more than a 12- to 14-day supply in storage to power her industries, homes, and automobiles. Interruptions in the flow of oil from the Middle East quickly would lead to a slowdown and then to a halt in the productivity of this oil-poor land.

3. Twilight of the hydrocarbon age. The United States and other countries unquestionably are running out of the cheap, con-

---

[3] The advice of Dr. Roy Amara, president of the Institute for the Future, was especially helpful in the process of selecting some of the developments that seem likely to shape the next two or three decades.

[4] About 20 percent of the NEA panelists were either foreign nationals or had had extensive experience overseas. In general, they felt that most of the dozen developments foreseen here had a direct bearing on the *entire* global community, not just the United States.

venient sources of energy, such as oil and natural gas, that have powered the growth of modern industry. U.S. consumption of oil has increased fivefold in little more than 20 years, and in 1975 we consumed 18 million barrels daily, of which 10 million were imported.

Even assuming that we will not again be cut off from the Middle East oil, alternative sources of energy must be developed rapidly. The seriousness of the situation is illustrated by the fact that all proven U.S. reserves (including estimates of Alaskan and off-shore fields) *without imported oil* would last for fewer than 3,500 days at our present consumption rates. By the time children who are now in the first grade graduate from high school, all our oil would be gone if we were forced to rely solely on U.S. reserves. The same is true of natural gas. Coal is the only fuel of which we have a large reserve, and much research is needed before we learn how to convert it to an economical and nonpolluting substitute for natural gas and petroleum.[5]

Many people think of energy problems in terms of empty fuel tanks, cutbacks in home heating, or the stalled wheels of industry. One of the serious but seldom mentioned threats in natural gas and petroleum depletion is the way in which it endangers U.S. agricultural productivity. Not only are great quantities of fuel needed for farm machinery, but also approximately a ton of oil is needed to produce a ton of ammonium hydroxide, necessary for the manufacture of one of our most widely used fertilizers.

To sum up: While we still have time to do so, humans everywhere need to engage cooperatively in the research that will find ways to increase energy reserves by harnessing the power of the atom, of the sun, of the earth's thermal energy, of hydrogen as fuel, of the tides, or of the wind.

4. Re-examined concepts of growth. In the next two or three decades, we must continue to give careful thought to policies that will govern the use of the earth's dwindling resources. Since these resources, with few exceptions, are not self-renewing, the need to be more frugal will inevitably lead to a new interpretation of the

---

[5] Some estimates indicate that the potential energy represented by U.S. coal reserves is double that of the energy potential of Middle East oil. Even so, coal supplies, too, could be depleted during the lifetimes of children born in 1976.

meaning of *growth*. Because of demands for more and more material goods in all quarters of the earth, we are obliged by the constraints of environment to seek a balance between social and economic objectives that serve the general welfare and the need to attain a dynamic equilibrium between human needs and the exploitation of resources. In the United States, we are just now discarding the popular myth that our resources and capital are inexhaustible. The task now before us is to define *constrained* growth, to recognize that there are limits to the earth's bounty, and to make the decisions and trade-offs involved in striking a balance between environmental protection and the material things which humans exploit the biosphere to obtain.

This will not be an easy task because, as Wilson Riles of the Project Pre-Planning Committee pointed out, "The American belief in unlimited natural resources . . . goes back to Colonial times. The destruction of white pine forests in Maine, the strip mining of West Virginia, the creation of the Midwest 'Dust Bowl' during the Great Depression," Riles noted, "all symbolize the American belief in [inexhaustible] resources and the misuse of our environment."[6]

5. *Increased crowding, lingering hunger.*   No one knows precisely how many people are alive today, but the world certainly is becoming more crowded. A ballpark estimate provided by demographers is that in 1975, or early in 1976, global population sped past the four billion mark.

Whatever their number may be, human beings are reproducing at a staggering rate. In 10,000 B.C. there were perhaps 12 million humans—about the same number as live in the greater London area today. Not until the mid-19th century did world population pass the billion mark—but now it is estimated that our numbers will increase by one billion in the nine years between 1985 and 1994. The net increase in the number of mouths to be fed each day is 200,000.[7] Every ten days two million persons (the equivalent of a

---

[6]Letter to the writer dated July 30, 1976. More will be made of this point in Chapter V when cardinal premises anticipating education for the year 2001 are discussed.

[7]Of this figure, approximately one quarter are born in five countries: China, India, Indonesia, Pakistan, and Bangladesh.

city the size of Houston, Texas) are added to the human load carried by the planet. Every four days the number of babies born is greater than the population of Montana or South Dakota.

The rapid, uneven regional growth of populations has greatly aggravated the hunger problem, a tragic situation, which directly or indirectly led to the death of a million persons in 1975 and to the severe malnutrition of as many as ten million more. In the present as well as the future, careful thought and family planning are essential if current explosive population increases are to be defused. Father Hesburgh, in a sad footnote to the problem of starvation, described the permanent brain damage as well as physical stunting that results from malnutrition during the prenatal period or in the early years of life.

Panel members who addressed themselves to the population–hunger equation—and most of them did—repeatedly made clear that they based their visions of a better world on the assumption that there would be, and had to be, a leveling-off in the human numbers game either before 2000 A.D. or shortly thereafter.

Assumptions vary as to how much food the average person really needs. Estimates vary as to how much food is available in a given year, and, as we noted earlier, we are not quite sure just how many people there are. Nonetheless, it is perfectly clear that food is distributed unevenly, with the rich eating more and the poor much less. Also, there is evidence that the world is losing ground in its continuing effort to feed its billions. Population is increasing at 2 percent a year. So are planetary food supplies—but problems of distribution, spoilage, pilferage, and greater per capita demand are combining to make this less than a *true* 2 percent increase.

6. Continued pressure for human equity. The problems of population growth and the tragedy of needless hunger lead directly to another probable feature of the later 1970's and the 1980's: continued pressure for a better economic deal and improved status for "have-not" humans. Members of the panel viewed with deep concern the inequitable resource division between the United States and much of the rest of the world. As Father Hesburgh phrased it, "Someone has said that the world couldn't stand [the consumption of] two Americas. I am not sure that it can stand one! . . . It is almost obscene the way so many millions of Americans are overfed."

Not all panel members' reactions to the challenges of economic equity were equally vehement, but there was little dissent over the point that excessive consumption and waste of food in this country by those affluent enough to afford it was not only harmful to the health of Americans but also damaging to our image overseas.

Within the boundaries of the United States, stress was placed on the need for redistribution of economic and political power and for further assaults on discrimination against ethnic minorities. Governor Castro, for instance, said, "I think we should add equality as the eighth cardinal principle, thus giving this fundamental human right a separate and distinct emphasis of its own."

With regard to the third and fourth worlds, members expressed the hope that the United States could help developing nations by means of a massive effort to increase their productivity. In other words, the NEA panel recognized both the fact of interdependence and the need—through dynamic reciprocity—for cooperation to reduce what Daniel P. Moynihan colorfully labeled "the politics of resentment and the economics of envy"[8] which have hampered American goals and policies in the UN.

The emerging role of women and the continuing need for equity in their lives and careers was stressed by a number of participants. Helvi Sipilä, widely recognized for her leadership during International Women's Year, was uniquely eloquent in her stand on the importance of enhancing the status of women in many developing countries.

7. *Increasing demands from less developed countries for a new economic order.* More subtle and less visible than current pressures for greater equity for the third and fourth worlds is the desire on the part of these have-not nations for a new economic *order,* not merely a new *deal.* At least since 1974, these nations simply have not been satisfied with "the patching up of the existing system to compensate the poor for the disadvantages they suffer under it."[9]

A careful reading of the proceedings of a recent meeting of the UN Conference on Trade and Development, when stripped of its

---

[8]*Commentary,* March 1975.
[9]*The Washington Post,* September 17, 1975.

rhetoric, clearly indicates that the most important objective the developing nations have is to increase their proportionate share of the world's industrialized production by 25 percent in the next 25 years. Since their present industrial level is 7 percent, this represents an enormous increase of over 200 percent, thus posing an important threat to the industrially developed nations.[10] Such a "new economic order" could be particularly devastating to Britain or Japan as they are forced into competition with developing nations which have the raw materials and cheap labor that these two countries lack. It also could be a problem for the United States and other nations (Canada, USSR, Brazil, the People's Republic of China, and so on) that are blessed with natural resources *and* an established industrial capacity. To illustrate the nature of the problem, according to Arthur H. Okun of the Brookings Institution, the United States needs a real growth rate of about 4 percent in the gross national product (GNP) to keep unemployment from rising above its already high level.[11] If, in the years ahead, the less developed world approaches 25 percent of the gross world product, and the industrialized socialist countries increase their GNP's, there will almost inevitably be radical changes in the status of the industrialized capitalist world with respect to such elements as power, unemployment, inflation, political stability, and the like.[12]

Once we have more clearly defined the meaning of equity—and we are beginning to make some progress in this direction—it will be important to make sure that decisions based on social justice and consensus really work. Panel participants were in general agreement that this process should begin within the United States itself and then extend outward in our economic and political relationships with other nations.

As the United States seeks, along with the rest of the industrialized nations, to cope with the challenge of domestic and

---

[10] See UN documents A/PV 2326-2349.

[11] Okun, a distinguished economist, also contends that much more than a 4 percent annual growth in the GNP is needed to reduce unemployment (*The New York Times,* July 2, 1975, p. 43).

[12] Geoffrey Barraclough has made a richly detailed study of the prospects for a new economic order. See "The Haves and the Have-nots," *The New York Review of Books,* May 13, 1976.

world poverty, our nation will continue to face the task of increasing our efficiency and that of other nations in producing the world's foodstuffs and manufactured goods so that there will be more of them to share. As redistribution of wealth and power continues, world stability in the 1990's may be substantially determined by our success during the 1980's in increasing productivity and in resolving conflicting claims to the world's fossil fuels, minerals, ocean harvests, and previously accumulated wealth.

8. *Troubled international waters.* While recognizing the need for effective peace-keeping through international agreements and machinery, panel participants were not particularly sanguine about prospects for international order before the 21st century. As social scientist Elise Boulding put it, "If you consider the Celtic League image, what the Bretons are thinking, what the Basque Separatists are thinking, and what other tribal movements are seeking as their image of the future, we will have to put together a very different world from the one we have now." The aspirations, needs, and problems with which the planet abounds seem certain to test the "leadership of ideas" that our best social, economic, and political innovators can provide.

But the international problems of the world community are too vital and too complex to be dismissed with a glib phrase. As one member of the NEA Project Pre-Planning Committee pointed out, the role of education in moving us toward a true community of nations is not likely to succeed if it fails "to deal with the impact of oppressive police states such as the Soviet Union and its satellites; the Union of South Africa, capable of murdering rioting . . . students; the growing dictatorship in India; the dictatorial governments in South America [including] a particularly brutal regime in Brazil."[13]

9. *Changing concepts of work and leisure.* While changing work roles and shifting patterns of leisure-time activities seem certain to be important facets of the future, panel members disagreed about the future role of both of these concepts in Americans' lives. Some of them saw less leisure ahead in an era in which a

---

[13]Letter to the writer from Wilson Riles dated July 30, 1976.

diminished supply of energy could lead to more labor-intensive production—a return to a greater physical toil in the factory, the home, and on the farm—at least until new, safe and improved sources of energy become available. However, a majority of participants in the NEA inquiry felt that energy-saving practices (turning off idle machines, saving on light and heat) would steadily increase in our homes and in industry which, in 1975, consumed 41 percent of the energy used in the United States. Presumably, with parsimony and in the absence of another oil embargo, the energy-intensive U.S. economy can theoretically support time for leisure during the next 20 or 25 years. However, "work" and "leisure" may acquire new meanings between 1976 and 1996 as values and perceptions change.[14]

Other factors that are likely to influence both leisure and work in the United States include an aging population (10.6 percent past 65) capable of work beyond present-day retirement ages, lower birthrates (leading to a 3-to-1 ratio of adults to children by the year 2000), the likelihood of increased production through greater efficiency, uncertain economic conditions, the prospect of even more women in the work force, and continued inflation that would motivate more workers to hold down two or even three jobs.

10. Governmental debt and capital deficits. The British Labor government's painful 1976 decision to cut public spending by 12 percent, with educational expenditures cut most of all, is a grim reminder of two financial problems that loom on the horizon. One of these is mounting debt; the other is a shortage of capital for investment purposes. The cost of U.S. welfare programs between 1964 and 1974 increased 738 percent, and (in the 1975–1976 fiscal year) Medicare, veterans' benefits, and comparable subsidized programs totalled $116 billion. Data from the U.S. Office of Education indicate that public and private educational costs—local, state, and federal—passed the $108 billion mark during the fiscal year 1975–1976.

As reduced paychecks indicate, Social Security costs are increasing, too, and there are no immediate prospects of a reverse trend.

---

[14]These changes are elaborated in Chapter IV where the worthy use of leisure, one of the seven cardinal principles of education, is discussed in some detail.

Particularly toward 1996 or 2001—an interval during which the U.S. postwar baby boom population begins to retire—cost problems will multiply. While there were only 22 million Americans of 65 or older during 1974, their numbers will increase to 31 million—an increase of 41 percent—by 2001.

The potential lack of investment capital for government programs and for borrowing by the business community also could pose a problem, especially if interest rates return to higher levels.

11. Problems of governance and threats to freedom. Panel members frequently expressed the opinion that we are only just beginning to develop the know-how needed to manage our affairs from the local to the international levels. Because of uncertainty about what functions should be performed at each governmental level, the power to be delegated at each level and the structure and size of each unit is unclear.

In the troubled times through which the country is passing, we have a special need to recognize and to repair governmental flaws. We also need to address the problem of how a broader base of citizen participation can be achieved through what Alvin Toffler has called "anticipatory democracy." In the process we need to devise really effective ways to avoid racial frictions, political conflict, and Balkanization or fragmentation, and more fully recognize individual rights in a polycultural and multiethnic society. Finally, we need to be aware of the spectre of "regulated freedom," the danger of bureaucratic restrictions that could result as the promise of social welfare leads to arbitrary limits being placed on personal freedom.

Imbedded in the question of freedom is an educational dilemma—the long-standing enigma of how to obtain the important output of superior minds without creating an elite of scientists, politicians, social planners and commentators, military specialists, business executives, and so on. Patently, the United States and the world desperately need a cadre of "global servants" (as panelist Robert J. Havighurst called them), dedicated to serving the common good. Most elites, whether in ancient Rome or in contemporary societies, tend to develop entrenched privileges and to be self-perpetuating—if only through the advantages to which the children of an elite are exposed. Hopefully, a genuinely equitable body of educational, social, and economic opportunities in the United States will blunt the horns of the elitist–egalitarian dilemma, which is nonetheless likely to be a major educational concern during the 1976–2001 interval.

12. A postextravagant society. Because of the combined impact of recession and unemployment, the 40 percent decline in the purchasing power of the dollar in ten years, the alarm over resource depletion, and severe international problems, many Americans share an uneasy feeling that the good old days are gone—that the years of U.S. affluence have ended. Gloomy seers such as Robert Heilbroner[15] and Robert Bundy have warned that even modest levels of affluence may be unattainable by 1985 or 1990, that shortages will be chronic, and that by 2001 the United States will show signs of increasing wear and tear as the country is lived in for a longer time by more people.

NEA panelists, by contrast, were much more often sanguine than pessimistic. While they envisioned continued economic discomfort, they also felt that many major problems related to plundered resources could be tempered by reasonable parsimony, by a prudent balance in export–import policies, and by a gradual phaseout of the "throw-away society" that has developed in the past two decades. They viewed recycling and "voluntary simplicity" in lifestyles as remedies for many potential shortages, and "voluntary frugality" was suggested both to improve over-rich American diets and to stretch foodstuffs that are temporarily in short supply.

To summarize: Despite dissent as to how to reach the desired goal, a substantial number of panelists contended that Americans could avoid a grim postaffluent society by striving now to create a postextravagant era during the next quarter century. They strongly supported the belief that we can back away from debilitating forms of exponential growth and yet avoid arbitrary limits to growth, thus raising the subsistence level of tens of millions as rapidly as possible. Hopefully then, as we approach 2000 or 2020 A.D., the present industrial society, which has maintained itself by ever-

---

[15]For an updated statement of Professor Heilbroner's views, see his "Second Thoughts on the Human Prospect" in the British journal *Futures,* February 1975, pp. 31–40.

increasing growth, will be replaced by one that has attained a better balance among humans and their use of resources.

More thoughtful planning (one panelist called it, "future-think") that shows greater awareness of the problems an interdependent world is likely to encounter, is a benign force already shaping the lives of millions. The study of the future promises to be even more influential during the last quarter of the century. Long-range planning and legislation intended to protect the biosphere provide an excellent example of our increasing need, both nationally and locally, of present efforts to insure environmental protection. Extensive research aimed at devising new energy sources reflects another of our attempts to anticipate human needs in the next millennium. Presumably, there will be even wider recognition of the fact that the future is not a new continent to be *explored* but a new world to be *created*.

THE FUTURE-FOCUSED IMAGES OF U.S. YOUTH.   Because of the NEA's commitment to youth, the Pre-Planning Committee and members of the Association's Bicentennial Committee unanimously urged that students of secondary school age be interviewed to obtain their perceptions of the future. Therefore, a multiethnic sample of 95 boys and girls (chosen for social maturity and verbal skills) also were interviewed and taped.[16]

On the whole, the young respondents were cautiously optimistic, hopeful that human relations on a planetary basis could be improved, and confident in the capacity of people everywhere to solve their problems. Except for one youth who doubted that we would be around 20 years from now because of a devastating nuclear war, the respondents accepted the idea that great and generally benign changes would occur and that life also would become more and more complicated. They expressed considerable concern over the need to improve the government and political processes, gave evidence of a strong internationalist spirit, and showed a clear awareness of dangers in pollution, hunger, population trends, and resource depletion.

---

[16]For a more detailed report on the NEA youth interviews, see Catherine McKenzie Shane, "Coping, Caring, Communicating: Youth Looks at the Future," *Phi Delta Kappan* 58: 117–121; September 1976.

Each group of young people interviewed expressed the fear that the next quarter century would bring into being a society in which materialism and technology would become increasingly dominant. Some spoke nostalgically of "a return to the simple life of our fore-fathers," although none could identify what this simple life was. One girl, a New York City senior, had already made plans for her simple future life—"away from it all" on a horse farm.

A conservative tone marked the social, religious, and political opinions they expressed. The major exception to their conservative stance was in regard to schooling, where they called for substantial evolutionary, and sometimes revolutionary, innovations. Many of the changes the students proposed are quite congruent with the 28 educational premises winnowed from the adults' tapes. (See Chapter V.)

The roles the young people saw for themselves in 1996 were of particular interest. Well over half of them cast themselves in some type of professional or service activity—white-collar workers in a postindustrial society. Little interest was evident in executive, managerial, or ownership roles, and there was only a scattered interest in factory or sales jobs, usually as employment of a transient nature.

One of the seven subgroups of the youth sample consisted of male "drop-ins" in their late 'teens who had voluntarily re-enrolled in a special urban school program, of which they spoke most highly. Their responses revealed limited imagination with respect to change and the future. Their career plans were fuzzy and they had only the haziest ideas of a personal role 20 years ahead. However, the young men proved to be the most enthusiastic learners inter-viewed when they discussed their school, its teachers, and the per-sonalized programs of instruction.

Regardless of the background of the U.S. teenagers interviewed, one phenomenon was noted. The role that every boy and girl fore-saw was more or less a reflection of a *present* life-style. While recog-nizing the sweep of change, youth apparently do not envision themselves going through any major personal or socioeconomic upheavals or mutations resulting from energy crises, pollution, or social unrest. They envision a future that is a good bit like the present but much improved through better human relations.

For purposes of contrast and comparison, a dozen university-bound Scottish boys and girls from six preparatory schools were taped. Despite the limited nature of the sample, it was nonetheless notable that these young people from the Strathclyde region (Glasgow) were quite insular in their thinking. They displayed a limited world view while voicing their concern for the future of Scotland and for the university system represented by Oxford and Cambridge and the major Scottish universities. After the years they had spent studying English literature, Latin and Greek, science and mathematics, and preparing weekly essays, one can understand their interest in the traditional order of things as distinct from the strong service-centered focus of the majority of the U.S. sample.

The young Scots also served as an important reminder that even in a sample of teenagers with a shared language, there remain major cultural and attitudinal differences with which the young will need to cope as they meet on the international scene.

WILL THERE BE A REAPPRAISAL OF THE SOCIAL SYSTEMS OF THE INDUSTRIALIZED WORLD? What social scientists call "lead indicators" apparently foreshadow our human futures. At the moment, these indicators suggest considerable dissatisfaction with the society which, during the past century, has developed along with the industrial system of developed countries. Among the clues that suggest this dissatisfaction are the environmental protection movement and the recent eruption of "rights" groups working on behalf of women, the young, the old, homosexuals, ethnic minorities, and so on. Another token of discontent is the job alienation so vividly portrayed in Studs Terkel's book *Working.* Still other omens of social malaise are found in the general lack of confidence in politicians, mistrust of the practices of governmental and military agencies, and in widespread concern about dubious business practices such as the bribes or huge "commissions" paid out by several multinational corporations.

Patterns of discontent and the reassessment of industrial society which many panel members believed are surfacing appear in many forms. Testimony from the NEA tapes suggests that the discontent is reflected in alienation, purposelessness, sexual laxity, maladjustments, crime and violence, religious cultism, and self-indulgence. More important than the rising tides of dissatisfaction is the matter of where they may carry us.

At least three future possibilities were mentioned by panelist

Willis Harman. On the one hand, new directions may lead to *reforms* that will restore lost credibility in our social institutions and that will defuse potentially explosive problems without discarding the traditional U.S. political and industrial framework. On the other hand, unrest may lead to governmental *repression* deemed necessary by political leaders because they feel that dissent has begun seriously to threaten social and economic stability. A third alternative future might materialize with a new *"moral society"* developing after 10 to 20 extremely disruptive years.

If the third development should occur, we may enter a 21st century guided by an ecological ethic, stabilized by greater justice in resource distribution, and made more livable by maturing human-relations skills, including the art of reaching a social consensus. In such a world, one would hope, the science and technology on which we have grown to depend would be in the process of becoming the servants of enlightened social policies rather than the arbiters of truth for an impersonal industrial society.

CHAPTER III
HUMAN POTENTIAL IN
AN INTERDEPENDENT WORLD

SOME REASONS FOR OPTIMISM IN A TROUBLED WORLD. Despite harsh realities and such potentially disruptive forces as a major famine that might confront the world community during the next 25 years, members of the NEA International Panel were cautiously optimistic about the human prospect in 1996 or 2001. These able men and women showed their capacity to grasp the complex relationships of an interdependent world and to make moral and intellectual sense of the data which the present era is producing. Therefore, their positive feelings about the future and about future education would seem to merit careful attention.

The general consensus among panelists was that we could confront the future with confidence because humans have long demonstrated a remarkable capacity to cope with a multitude of problems. Life has rarely been easy in the wide range of environments—from frigid zones to tropics—that uncompromising nature has provided during the past 50,000 years. Panelists agreed that our next task, now that we have partly tamed these environments, is to tame ourselves by using wisely the imposing array of knowledge and skills at our disposal. Despite some human error, consultants felt, we can find encouragement in the way the race already has achieved a proud record of accomplishments in agriculture, communication, transportation, education, industry, and other realms of human endeavor.

Some panel members also felt confident about the future because a rising level of social consciousness in the United States has prodded Americans toward many needed reforms and augurs well for the future. Looking back to 1900, one woman noted that children as young as eight were working up to 14 hours a day in coal mines, that women had no vote and only limited property rights, that workers by the thousands died or were disfigured in industrial accidents, and that ethnic minorities were parodied or derided on the stage and by the press. "Today," she went on, "we have public health programs, minimum wages, legislation to promote the laborer's safety, as well as aid for dependent children, the aged, and the poor; and various rights are assured to minorities. More has been accomplished to serve human welfare in the past 75 years than was accomplished in 75 previous centuries. I see these gains being retained, refined, and extended by 2001." Other panelists spoke of our increased insight into the pressing economic needs of the have-not world and of environmental and consumer protection movements as signs that Americans were retaining their ability to cope with changing times and emerging needs.

A third note of optimism preserved in the NEA tapes reflected confidence in the ability of people everywhere increasingly to learn to use science and technology with greater skill and prudence. The communications satellite, Telstar, has demonstrated how a few hundred pounds of copper can do the work of literally thousands of tons of copper cable. The seabed mining of self-replacing mineral nodules represents yet another breakthrough—a development promising to provide millions of tons of nickel, copper, manganese, and cobalt just when these resources were in danger of falling into short supply or under the control of cartels.

Social inventiveness also has been improving—thus providing a fourth reason for confidence in the future. International machinery to help defuse explosive problems, social science research that has improved cross-cultural insights, and human welfare legislation all serve to illustrate the point.

Furthermore, we have only begun on a worldwide basis to exploit education as a means of increasing the intellectual horsepower of people of all ages. Let us put this another way: a trend is not human destiny. Through the teaching–learning process, on a worldwide scale there are no known problems which humankind cannot overcome. As panelist Norman Cousins put it, "I'm an optimist because we don't yet know enough to be pessimistic!" Cousins' encouraging statement reminds us that humans have successfully outlasted the forecasts of many varieties of doomsayers—including both scientists and philosophers.

As remarked earlier, the panel members generally did not agree with the fear some writers express that even modest aspirations can not be fulfilled in the future and that shortages will become permanent. Panelists rejected the idea that oldsters would look back from 2001 to 1966 or 1976 and remember them as "the best of times." During his interview, David Rockefeller even anticipated the new, more optimistic Club of Rome policy, which favors "selective growth"; he commented that "reports from the Club of Rome based on the computerized treatment of trends that suggest we should have no more growth simply don't allow for the adaptability of humanity."[1]

Despite their positive outlooks, despite their certainty that our American society had no death wish, the panelists left little doubt that the mettle of the United States would be tested now that it has lost some of the status and most of the reflexive deference that its citizens enjoyed when travelling overseas in the 1950's. As many adolescent nations seek to find themselves and to achieve stability, Americans will need quickly to develop good-humored resignation to the frequent imperfections of these neighbors and of ourselves as we strive to live together in a climate of mutual respect and good will.

GUIDELINES FOR APPROACHING THE FUTURE. Either explicitly or by implication, the NEA panelists offered interesting advice to the readers of *Curriculum Change Toward the 21st Century* as to how they might most successfully confront the 25 years between 1976 and 2001.

1. Old beliefs and ideas must be re-examined. Since some of the axioms accepted by both the United States and other nations have become unworkable and even dangerous because the nature of survival behavior has changed in recent years, panelists urged that old values and beliefs be re-examined.

At one time, as Lester R. Brown pointed out, families of unlimited size helped tribal groups to prosper; now population pressures have turned unlimited reproduction into a serious threat to the future of humanity. Panelists also rejected as dangerous and indefensible the belief that U.S. resources are inexhaustible and

---

[1] *Newsweek,* April 26, p. 84; *Time,* April 26, p. 56.

that it was the "right" of Americans in a free enterprise system to exploit them without hindrance for personal gain.

2. There is no "surprise-free" future. The writer once asked Kenneth Boulding, author of *The Meaning of the 20th Century,* whether there was *any* statement about the future that was categorically true. "Yes," Boulding replied, "there is. You can be sure that our tomorrows will be full of surprises!" Again, the NEA panelists frequently noted that there was no such thing as a "surprise-free" future and that educational planning must remain flexible.

3. We "create" the future. Although old axioms are no longer uniformly reliable, although the years ahead are likely to be enlivened by unpredictable developments, human destiny always has been and will continue to be largely what human beings make it. Moon landings, Martian probes, successful attacks on diseases such as polio, improvements in cross-cultural insights and international relationships, our initial efforts to contain the more appalling problems of pollution—these and many other accomplishments are all evidences that support an important point: we create the future by what we do—or fail to do. The future is not an endless road we are condemned inexorably to follow. It is a fan-shaped array of alternative possibilities. It is essential to remember that we create the future. The role of education in the process is potentially so important that it is difficult to overstate its contribution as the world's nations move through the human revolution of the present.

4. "Facts" can be the enemy of truth. As we engage in the processes of creating educational changes, we need to be as certain as we can be that the data on which we rely are reliable. In the 1930's, for instance, many parents and educators alike assumed that IQ was fixed and virtually unchangeable. Now we believe that what we measure as intelligence is a quality that is *developed* through learning experiences. To use another illustration, at one time most psychologists erroneously thought of the mind as analogous to a muscle that could be strengthened through the discipline of exercise; hence, young people memorized poetry or prose passages, learned rote definitions, and so on, to "strengthen" their minds. Other examples are abundant. Educators need to be sure to avoid accepting unexamined assumptions as facts as they design schools for an era of rapid change and complexity.

5. *Fields of human knowledge overlap and interact.* Developments in chemistry began to have a bearing on education when it was demonstrated in the 1960's that mind, memory, and mood are influenced by various kinds of drugs. The use of lasers for projecting three-dimensional images, a development in the realm of physics, may make available to teachers instructional aids that almost undetectably simulate reality. These and analogous developments suggest that the future—including the future of schooling—will be mediated by the impact of developments in one field of study or inquiry upon others. Teachers will, as a consequence, need to raise the rim of their vision to include more than classroom know-how in their preservice and inservice activities.

6. *The time for positive action is limited.* When they suggested attitudes and stances for anticipating and learning to cope with tomorrow's problems and to take advantage of new opportunities, the panelists usually mentioned that the time available for meeting humankind's problems was brief. It would appear that social *decisions* related to domestic and international problems (energy shortages, resource depletion, widespread malnutrition) need to be reached by the mid-1980's. *Action* needs to be taken as soon thereafter as possible, and no later than, say, 1990, if the planet as a whole is to avoid a re-run of the more tragic aspects of the middle ages: tyranny, poverty, fear, ignorance.

It is in this context of optimism, of urgency, and of the need to re-examine values that the following chapters—chapters directly concerned with educational goals, premises to guide reforms in U.S. schooling, and classroom practice—should be read.

CHAPTER IV
EDUCATIONAL GOALS
FOR A NEW MILLENIUM

Education for living in a world in transition, including schooling that anticipates the 21st century, requires more than an image of what the year 2001 will demand. It requires an examined body of educational goals or objectives which are consistent with and supportive of our images of the world 25 years hence.

BACKGROUND. As indicated in Chapter I, the NEA—as one of its investments in better educational futures—sought to determine whether or not the seven cardinal principles of education promulgated in 1918 continued to be valid goals after almost 60 years. Before revisiting the cardinal principles, it seems appropriate to remember that Americans searched for new directions in education even before the republic was founded. For example, in April 1635, in the new Massachusetts colony, the Boston Citizens' Schooling Committee employed a certain Philemon Purmont to instruct the young in a public school. The down-to-earth flavor of the goals of the New England parents of 341 years ago was made clear in old records because of the emphasis they directed Master Purmont to place on the three R's.

During the 1660's and 1670's, the command of subject matter and skills continued to be an educational goal, if one is to judge by the surviving description of objectives for the curriculum of Boston's "free schools to teach the children of the poor." A century later, in 1789, a "Committee of Eminent Bostonians," headed by Samuel Adams, was to provide new directions. The "new system of

An abridged version of Chapter IV, "The Seven Cardinal Principles Revisited," appeared in *Today's Education,* 65:57–72; September–October 1976.

education" recommended by the committee advocated the radical principal that public education should be distributed in proportion to the needs of the people. Also, and at public expense, the committee provided for the education of girls if they were seven or older and if they previously had been taught to read!

Since its establishment as the National Teachers Association[1] in Philadelphia during 1857, the NEA has vigorously continued the early American tradition of seeking and reassessing or reframing educational goals. Judging by the record, the Association may well have been *the* most important source of statements or professional reports with a bearing on goals and on new educational directions for the United States. Because they were so influential, it seems fitting to recall a few of the Association's historically significant committees and their pronouncements.

PAST NEA COMMITTEE REPORTS OF INFLUENCE IN U.S. EDUCATION: THE COMMITTEE OF TEN.

Among the distinguished NEA committees that have dealt with issues and goals, one of the most influential was the Committee of Ten. With Charles W. Eliot as chairman, the committee members were directed to establish standards for the secondary school. In 1893, a year after the committee was established, its report was published. Among its high-impact proposals was a new unit system for determining credit, a six-year elementary school with fixed time schedules for instruction in the various skill subjects, and advocacy of formal mental discipline based on the faculty psychology learning theory which was then popular.[2]

The committee identified six major objectives, including that of training the pupils' powers of observation, reasoning, and expression. An historically interesting and revealing paragraph of the report read as follows:

---

[1]In 1870, the National Teachers Association revised its constitution and became the National Education Association. In 1906, it was incorporated by an act of Congress as the National Education Association of the United States.

[2]Faculty psychology assumed that there were mental faculties capable of being trained: memory, observation, reason, judgment, etc. Just as a muscle might be improved by exercise, it was assumed, so memory could be improved by memorizing, or observation by observing.

> As studies in language and in the Natural sciences are best adapted to cultivate the habits of observation; as mathematics are the traditional training of the reasoning faculties; so history and its allied branches are better adopted than any other studies to promote the invaluable mental power which we call judgment.[3]

The Eliot report was destined to influence school practice and policies for years to come, and some of its recommendations remain with us yet.

THE COMMITTEE OF FIFTEEN. During 1893 the NEA set up a Committee of Fifteen. (Originally ten members were proposed, but five more were added to avoid confusion resulting from *two* Committees of Ten!) This committee focused on the organization of city school systems, on the coordination of studies in the elementary school, and on the preparation of teachers.

In certain ways the Committee of Fifteen's 1895 report sharply departed from that of the Committee of Ten. While continuing to accept "mental discipline," the committee unanimously adopted the almost contemporary proposition that

> The civilization of the age—the environment into which the child is born—should determine the objects of study, to the end that the child may gain an insight into the world in which he lives and command of its resources such as is obtained by helpful cooperation with his fellows.[4]

A wry inference as to the status of teachers 80 years ago may, by the way, be drawn from another of the committee's recommendations, namely, that grade school teachers be obliged to obtain a high school diploma before they are employed.

THE COMMITTEE OF TWELVE AND THE COMMITTEE ON THE SIX-YEAR COURSE OF STUDY. Between 1895 and 1909, several additional reports from NEA committees enlivened the educational scene. After four years of deliberation,

---

[3]Charles W. Eliot, chm., *Report of the Committee of Ten on Secondary School Studies.* New York: American Book Co., 1894. p. 168.

[4]National Educational Association, *Addresses and Proceedings, 1895.* St. Paul, Minnesota: the Association, 1895. p. 235.

the Committee of Twelve came up with more than a dozen proposals that were both widely discussed and influential. One of these urged that the seventh grade become a part of the high school to improve the quality of instruction—a suggestion that led to the birth of the first junior high schools in 1910 when Berkeley, California, and Columbus, Ohio, almost simultaneously adopted the new idea. This committee also seemed to anticipate some aspects of career education by recommending that secondary schools serve as "schools of the people" in addition to preparing students to meet college entrance requirements.

An NEA committee concerned with a six-year course of study reported each year from 1907 through 1909. This group of scholars made the somewhat anomalous and contradictory proposal that high school should be six years in length in order to prepare youth more adequately for college. In retrospect, this recommendation seems self-defeating since it reduced the time to be spent in elementary school. In other words, the proposed trade-off threatened to reduce the time spent readying the child either for secondary education or for the world of work, which at that time virtually all Americans entered when they left "the grades."[5] For years to come the profession was to be divided by the issue that the committee raised: Should elementary schools be responsible for well-rounded development of children or should they concentrate on the academic tools deemed necessary for subsequent success in high school?

THE COMMITTEE ON ECONOMY OF TIME.   In 1908, the National Council on Education (an NEA creation) appointed the Committee on Economy of Time to tackle a problem that has retained its vigor for 70 years: the problem of the crowded curriculum and what to do about it. The importance of the group's report resides partly in the domino effect that its conclusions had on U.S. education.

In addition to stirring up the curriculum field, the report moti-

---

[5]As late as 1940, census data indicated that *half* of the U.S. adult population had not gone on to high school. In 1918, just before the universalization of secondary education, only one child in three went to high school and only three out of 100 earned a diploma.

vated a seven-year curriculum study by the Department of Superintendence. Furthermore, it eventuated in two distinguished and influential curriculum yearbooks of the National Society for the Study of Education, yearbooks which reflect the early phases of the so-called scientific movement in curriculum development.[6]

THE COMMISSION ON THE REORGANIZATION OF SECONDARY EDUCATION.[7] Of all NEA-sponsored studies, probably none was more visible, more widely studied and quoted, or more remembered for its impact than the 1918 report of the Commission on the Reorganization of Secondary Education, the report in which the seven cardinal principles made their first appearance. The decision of the NEA to study and possibly to reframe these principles in 1976 is eloquent testimony to their enduring role as an important body of objectives or goals for U.S. education.

Established in 1913, the commission was destined to carry education in the United States in new directions. For one thing, the membership included several junior professors who were innovative young rebels of the era. (Among those whose names are still widely remembered: Thomas H. Briggs, Alexander Inglis, James F. Hosic, William H. Kilpatrick, and Otis W. Caldwell.) Secondly, the group included seasoned, tough-minded practitioners such as the Chairman, C. D. Kingsley, a state high school supervisor, and P. P. Claxton, the U.S. Commissioner of Education.

---

[6]These 1927 yearbooks were *Curriculum Making: Past and Present* and *The Foundations of Curriculum Making.* Harold O. Rugg was the chairman of the Committee on Economy of Time.

[7]Although the work of the Commission of the Reorganization of Secondary Education was particularly memorable, many other NEA-appointed groups left important footprints in the sands of time. Had space permitted, the following units appointed between 1921 and 1946 surely would have merited attention: Commission of Reorganization of Elementary Education (1921–1923), Commission on the Curriculum (1923–1929), Committee of 100 on Classroom Teachers' Problems (1923–1924), National Council of Education, National Council on Teacher Retirement, National Council on Safety Education, the Legislative and Federal Relations Division (1920), the Educational Policies Commission (1937) cosponsored by the AASA, the National Commission for the Defense of Democracy Through Education (1941), and the National Commission on Teacher Education and Professional Standards (1946).

In a sharp break with the Committee of Ten, the commission agreed that secondary education should be "determined by the needs of the society to be served, the character of the individuals to be educated, and the knowledge of educational theory and practice available," adding that "these factors are by no means static."[8]

In effect, the commission accepted "preparation for effective living" rather than "preparation for the college or university" as a guideline and rather substantially rewrote the rule book for U.S. education in response to the massive social and economic developments of the times, along with the implications for educational change which commission members identified.

While space precludes a detailed description of the discussions and conclusions out of which the cardinal principles were born, it is important to note that they were intended to help achieve "the ideal of democracy that the individual and society may find fulfillment each in the other."[9] After reaching this conclusion, the commission proceeded to analyze certain human activities—family, vocational, civic—and to identify seven objectives that should find a place in the education of every American boy and girl:

1. Health
2. Command of fundamental processes
3. Worthy home membership
4. Vocation
5. Civic education
6. Worthy use of leisure
7. Ethical character.

THE SEVEN CARDINAL PRINCIPLES OF EDUCATION REVISITED.   After their nearly 60 years of service to American education, it seems fitting to revisit the cardinal principles and to ask, Are these goals still valid? If so, what do they stand for in the contemporary world, and with what new or added meanings should they be endowed in a troubled, global community?

Those who recall the cardinal principles with nostalgia and affec-

---

[8]*Cardinal Principles of Secondary Education,* Bulletin #35. Washington, D.C.: Bureau of Education, 1918. p. 7.

[9]*Ibid.,* p. 9.

tion will be pleased to learn that all save a few members of the NEA International Panel feel that the seven goals have retained their usefulness and their importance even after the passage of nearly 60 years.[10] At the same time, educators who see a need for new goals and directions that anticipate a new millennium can take comfort from and find satisfaction in the fact that the panel also felt that the meanings originally associated with the cardinal principles were no longer adequate for learning and living in an interdependent human community. Some of the points the commission made in 1918 serve to illustrate the naiveté of the era.

For example, in interpreting the cardinal principle of "worthy home membership," the commission report stated that women, "even those planning for higher institutions," should have greater exposure to the household arts since after a few years "home making becomes their lifelong occupation."[11] The report associated the command of fundamental processes with "reading, writing, arithmetical computations, and the elements of oral and written expression." It construed health to mean the inculcation of "health habits," "a love for clean sport," and "physical activities" in schools where the surroundings "conform to the best standards of hygiene and sanitation."[12]

Yet the original statement of principles contains some interesting examples of prescience that suggest the unusual thoughtfulness of the men and women who drew up the 1918 report. "Geography," we are told, "should show the interdependence of men while it shows their common dependence on nature," and "the ideals of American democracy and loyalty to them should be a prominent aim of civic education."[13] A further comment on civic education needs very little recasting to adapt it to the world of 1976:

---

[10]Back in 1966 the Research Division of the NEA asked "a scientifically selected cross section of the nation's public school teachers" if the principles were outmoded. (See NEA Research Division, "A New Look at the Seven Cardinal Principles of Education." *NEA Journal,* January 1967, pp. 53–54.) It is of historical interest to note that more than 85 percent of the respondents felt that they were a satisfactory list of major objectives. Now, a decade later, the International Panel gives them a newly evaluated lease on life as objectives for U.S. education.

[11]*Cardinal Principles of Secondary Education,* p. 12.

[12]*Loc. cit.*

[13]*Ibid.,* p. 14.

Civic education should consider other nations also. As a people we should try to understand their aspirations and ideals that we may deal more sympathetically and intelligently with the immigrant coming to our shores, and have a basis for a wiser and more sympathetic approach to international problems. Our pupils should learn that each nation, at least potentially, has something of worth to contribute to civilization, and that humanity would be incomplete without the contribution.[14]

Several members of the NEA panel not only addressed themselves to revising the principles for use in the years ahead but took time to analyze and to speculate about the original principles.[15] Among the interesting and important points they made are the following:

1. The original cardinal principles did not distinguish between the general responsibilities for education and those that were best assumed by or shared with agencies such as the church, the community, and the family. Health, ethical character, worthy home membership, leisure activities, and civic skills often were influenced by or were influential in other arenas of life. The principles overpromised what the schools could do. We must now talk more sensibly about what schooling can actually accomplish.
2. The original principles did not anticipate how much learning we would require in the world of 1976. Now we must look at the total learning system. Except for literary, and possibly vocational efficiency, the cardinal principles are tasks for other educational agencies beyond the school walls. These include the home, church, and peer groups as well as mass media.
3. The principles, quite understandably, did not allow for the increasing need for lifelong adult education.
4. The 1893 Committee on Ten report focused on *subjects;* the cardinal principles focused on *goals.* The commission that created these seven principles, despite its impressive contribution, erred in two ways: first, in failing to recognize the role of other agencies in achieving the principles; and second, in mixing command of fundamental processes (subjects) with the other six. This has created the sort of problem situation in which "one committee of teachers sits somewhere devising social goals for

---

[14]*Loc. cit.*

[15]Ralph Tyler, Lawrence Cremin, and Sterling McMurrin are quoted or paraphrased in these four points.

the school district and talks in terms of global concepts while another committee is selecting or reorganizing the subjects. The trouble in our time is that the two have failed to meet."

These four statements do not imply that the principles have lost validity. They do, however, point to the need for re-examining and updating them. In the context of these remarks, attention is now directed to changes in the cardinal principles that panelists feel the passing years have made necessary.

THE SEVEN CARDINAL PRINCIPLES REIN-TERPRETED IN ANTICIPATION OF THE 21ST CENTURY. In 1927, the National Congress of Parents and Teachers incorporated the seven cardinal principles in their permanent platform. Subsequently, in a booklet published in consultation with the NEA,[16] the National Congress interpreted and slightly rephrased some of the principles.

This source and the original report of the Commission on the Reorganization of Secondary Education were used as referrents in determining the meanings that had attached themselves to the cardinal principles during the decade following their proclamation. By 1927, according to the National Congress, it had "become increasingly apparent that these [cardinal principles] were the objectives not only of the high school, but of all education."[17] The principles also were seen to be interwoven "as the intricate pattern of life is interwoven."

HEALTH. The original statement of the cardinal principles indicates that in 1918, the objective of health was to be sought through health instruction, inculcation of health habits, and physical activities. By 1927, mental and emotional fitness had been added, and the objective was restated to read "Health and Safety." The role of the home was mentioned along with the community's responsibility for sanitation and control of disease, for pure air,

---

[16]National Congress of Parents and Teachers, *Educating for Seven Point Lives.* Washington, D.C.: the Congress, 1927. 16 pp.

[17]*Ibid.,* p. 4. The original 1918 report also stated that the seven cardinal principles were applicable "to education as a whole" (p. 11).

playgrounds, and parks. Teachers were admonished to keep children clean, to train them in health habits, and to arrange for physical examinations.

In 1976 the NEA panelists made much more sophisticated statements regarding the health objective. They directed attention to the need for healthy interpersonal and intercultural attitudes, for instance, and made the point that children and youth need to be made aware that overconsumption can be as debilitating as underconsumption, and that both can affect one's behavior in similarly adverse ways. Also, they recommended a greater "social action" role for schools and other educational agencies in the health realm through directing learners' attention to the unhealthful aspects of imperfect U.S. life-styles and to environmental dangers such as air pollution, which, one consultant said, causes at least 60 percent of the cancer in the United States.

The panelists mentioned stress as a source of health problems and recommended a knowledge of "stress points" as a part of health education. They extended an understanding of dietary needs and problems beyond simple nutrition education to include such matters as dangers in food additives, in pollution, in faulty city planning, and in sanitary standards that are so low as to be inimical to health. And they urged continued efforts to improve drug education along with frank consideration, at appropriate age levels, of healthful family living including sexuality, problems that lead to divorce, and human needs for love and acceptance.

A number of panel members mentioned health as a transnational challenge. President Hesburgh of the University of Notre Dame commented that "it seems unreasonable for a few among the world's peoples to have the privilege of heart transplants while most people in the rest of the world don't see a doctor from birth to death." Also speaking in a cross-cultural context, Helvi Sipilä noted that "unless we take seriously the fate of women in developing countries, I don't think we can solve many of the other problems in the world. . . ."

One is led to infer from the NEA interview tapes that health not only remains an important objective but that as a major goal it has appreciably increased in scope. The goal emerged as "total mental, physical, and emotional health for the total person"; as tightly linked to environmental problems; as related to conditions in other countries on an interdependent planet; and as a responsibility to be assumed by all educational agencies, among which the schools remained extremely important.

COMMAND OF FUNDAMENTAL PROCESSES. Over the years the interpretation of "fundamental processes" has changed in a great many ways. While the panel vigorously reaffirmed the importance of proficiency in the three R's plus communication skills, it also identified a wide variety of skills other than those of language and numbers. The new and additional fundamental processes that were suggested sorted themselves into three categories:

1. Skill in humanistic processes, including human relations, group processes, and those skills based on cross-cultural and multiethnic insights
2. Neo-academic skills, including a knowledge of sources, the understanding and use of computer languages, and improved ability to cope with increasing specialization through a command of cross-disciplinary understandings
3. Anticipatory skills represented by (a) the ability to see relationships and to make correlations, (b) the skills of sorting, weighing, and then acting on data, (c) evaluating choices and making decisions wisely despite the current information and misinformation glut, and (d) understanding how power functions at various levels from neighborhoods to international capitals.

An examination of this formidable list of fundamental processes, extending as it does from literacy at one end of the spectrum to a functional understanding of power at the other, again tends to support the point made earlier that schools, as they now are constituted, are in need of closer cooperative relationships with other socioeducational agencies and with the home. But what *is* the nature of the home today? This provocative question leads directly to the panelists' ideas regarding the third cardinal objective.

WORTHY HOME MEMBERSHIP. When the panelists discussed worthy home membership, three distinct points became apparent. One was that the nature of the family is changing. Another, that the family is of great importance and is still needed in U.S. culture. A third dealt with the school's obligation to adapt themselves

to emerging home and family changes and, in the process, to re-think the meaning of "worthy."

Most-mentioned home changes included (a) the new opportu-nities and roles for women that have developed since the cardinal principles first appeared in 1918, (b) the impact of television, (c) the home's loss of influence on the individual, and (d) the increase in the variety of affinity groups that have gathered people together in a home relationship that often is quite unlike the traditional unit of father, mother, and two children. Some consultants spoke of the loss of self-worth experienced since the 1920's by children and youth as they found their roles as helpful, needed family members were diminished or wiped out by the changes in life-styles and in technology.

A social scientist, Elise Boulding, made the point that there was nothing really new about the fact that home and family changes oc-curred except for the fact that *we* are the ones involved in those that now are occurring. "We have had many kinds of social experiments (with a bearing on family life) in the course of human history," she continued, "including the single-sex and heterosexual communes that were abundant in the Middle Ages."

Despite novel living arrangements that have begun to compete with the traditional nuclear family, the panelists were like-minded in regarding some form of family membership as very important, and they expressed confidence in the indestructible nature of family bonds, irrespective of social change.

They felt, however, that affinity groups make important potential contributions in fulfilling the need for love and affection, in provid-ing a sheltering environment for the disadvantaged child, and in teaching the lesson of how to live with others in harmony and mutual respect. As Norman Cousins phrased it, family-type groups are "a closed ecosystem of rewarding, mutual interdependence."

While the family received a variety of accolades, its troubles also were the cause of concern. A number of suggestions bearing directly or indirectly on worthy home membership and on the improvement of home–school relations appear in interview transcripts. Among them are the following:

1. Heretofore, in a broad sense, the educational system has been a system comprised of the home, the workplace, the church, and the school. At present only the school continues to provide the same number of hours of educational experiences. The home has reduced its contribution. To illustrate this point, Ralph

Tyler commented that in 1960, 26 percent of mothers of school age children were in the labor force; in 1974, this figure had climbed to 51 percent. Many children now return to homes in which they have very little guidance, and this creates new responsibilities for other educational agencies.

2. One often-overlooked factor that bears on education is the power role of certain organized groups whose political and economic influence in serving their own interests can be detrimental to the welfare of such unorganized groups as children, youth, the unemployed, and old people.

3. In certain countries, the status of women must be improved further if there are to be families in which it is possible to achieve worthy home membership. To a considerable extent this generalization also applies in the United States, particularly with regard to minority groups.

4. Insofar as they have the time and ingenuity to do it, educational agencies, including schools, should make a carefully planned effort to help us rediscover the sense of well-being and pleasure that can be found in meaningful family living.

5. Because parents are so often involved in activities that take them out of the home setting, they should be encouraged by teachers to use the time they have with their children as "high quality time," that is, time planned to maximize the developmental significance of these parent–child contacts.

6. As a part of schooling, children and youth might well have more service-and-action type experiences that help them to sense what good home living involves—the nature of the responsibilities and duties as well as the privileges and opportunities. For example, Elise Boulding suggested that during their most vulnerable age—in their teens, "Children . . . might apprentice to mothers who've had new babies. Not only could these young people be useful to the mothers; we also would be getting more home-bound women to do their share of teaching."

If the cardinal principle of worthy home membership were to be rephrased to adapt it to 1976, probably most panel members would have agreed that it might better read "worthy *family* membership." This change would recognize that there are many affinity groups of value, in addition to the home cluster, in which children and youth might find family-type experiences.

VOCATION.   While the panelists recognized the importance of vocational skills, their concepts of contemporary vocational education were, for the most part, much more broad than those earning-a-livelihood goals that were voiced by the commission back in 1918. There was also a clear division of opinion in the panelists' replies. Some respondents felt that specific vocational training or preparation should continue to be carried on in the secondary and postsecondary school years. Others either stressed a general education as the best prerequisite to vocational success or argued that more and perhaps most vocational preparation should occur outside school walls. Harry Passow put it bluntly when he said, "Much that has been done in secondary education in the name of developing vocational skill might better have been accomplished outside the school."

Because of the range of viewpoints expressed, it seems desirable, in summarizing the tapes, to present or to contrast these views. In fairness, the thoughtful insights of the 1918 report should also be mentioned.

In its original form, *vocation* emphasized equipping the student to earn a living, to serve society through work, to "maintain the right relationships toward his fellow workers and society," and "as far as possible" to find personal development through vocation. The commission also recommended that those proficient in a given vocation should be employed as instructors and that apprentice-type experiences should be arranged either in or out of school.

The majority of the 1976 panelists tended to echo the thought that the best vocational education is a general education. Some of the views expressed are as follows:[18]

1. The problem [with regard to specific vocational skill training] in a changing society is to know what vocations are going to be required in the next 10 or 15 years.
2. A good general education should then be followed by teaching of specific skills.
3. The habit of *lifelong* learning is now, in a sense, a vocational skill.
4. Most vocational education can best be acquired outside of school.
5. Competence in problem solving has now become a requisite for vocational efficiency.
6. We need a "new vocational breed" that sees the implications *in their vocations* for combating pollution and other ecological problems.

---

[18]As noted earlier, a selection of the statements made during the taped interviews and the names of persons who made them are listed in the Appendix.

7. School should focus on the general requirements of all vocations and on serial or recurring preparation.
8. Vocational preparation must avoid locking people in the wrong jobs.

The panelists did not intend that their comments downgrade the importance of vocational education, but they did stress the notion that effective citizenship, vocational skills, and general education "are interrelated and more complex," according to Norman Cousins, "because life has become more complex and therefore more demanding."

A number of miscellaneous comments about vocational education can be summarized under the label "humanistic." That is, they concentrated on the panelists' views on how human welfare could best be served in preparation for the world of work. For instance:

1. Vocational skills must be carefully developed and productivity encouraged because, as wages spiral upward, the unskilled will continue to find themselves unemployed.
2. The school's prime tasks are to cultivate reason, increase knowledge, and facilitate self-realization, without which *vocation* loses much of its meaning.
3. In developing nations, less and less work is available to the untrained as populations increase, so vocational training is very much in the human interest.
4. Assuming that minimum wage guarantees appear in the United States during the next 20 years, it will be one of vocational education's challenges to help insure that competent, motivated, productive people are available with skills they can bring to a full employment program.
5. Independence and a feeling of self-worth depend on opportunities for exercising a vital ability. There is joy in reaching for excellence in some form. Vocational skills should help one to achieve these personal satisfactions.

CIVIC EDUCATION.   Despite the passage of time, it remains clear that the "cardinal principles" commission in its 1918 report recognized the vast importance of civic education. This recognition is reflected in the amount of coverage given to this goal—more than double that given any other objective except worthy home membership, which was a poor second.

Loyalty to the ideal of "civic righteousness" was emphasized along with a knowledge of social agencies and institutions and the "means and methods that will promote one [worthy] social end without defeating others." Ways of implementing changes through "habits of cordial cooperation in social undertakings" also were considered essentials for good citizenship. Superior citizenship, by the way, was singled out as "the dominant aim" of instruction in geography, history, civics, and economics at the secondary school level.

Understanding and respect for the ideals of democracy, as well as respect for the achievements, possibilities, and limitations of other nations were made clear in a statement that said in part: "[the] study of dissimilar contributions in the light of the ideal of human brotherhood should help to establish a genuine internationalism, free from sentimentality, founded on fact, and actually operative in the affairs of nations."[19]

The foresight of the commission statement with respect to civic education acquires fresh interest in the context of the goals or aims identified by the 1976 panelists. While one cannot say *plus ça change, plus c'est la même chose,* there are striking similarities between the 1918 report and the 1976 panel's thinking.

For one thing, tape after tape brings out the importance of world-mindedness. Repeatedly, one hears statements supporting "loyalty to the planet as well as to the nation," the "need for a world view," "world citizenship," and the need for "membership in much larger societies" or for recognizing that "citizenship is more than narrow chauvinism."

Some participants pointed out that civic education should make clear the need to narrow the gap between the industrially developed and the less developed nations, that a liberal education should give as much heed to national and international problems as to foreign language, and that the difficulties and challenges that exist in both laissez faire and planned societies should be presented.

Another rather frequent suggestion was that the young be made aware that the United States, if it wished to improve its moral posture and leadership in the world, could best do so by first cleaning up the littered nest of domestic troubles in Washington, D.C., and the 50 states. Another related point to be driven home through all educational media: we must work to build respect and support for leadership of integrity, "leadership that will not abdicate its

---

[19]*Ibid.,* p. 15.

responsibilities." Furthermore, if we wish to strengthen the integrity and health of leadership, we must strive even harder to keep special interest groups from putting pressure on government leaders in order to obtain from them the promise of special favors or preferential treatment in return for the support of these groups.

Other strong statements, perhaps mirroring contemporary political and social malaise, centered around power. An overseas participant—a Scottish professor—stressed the need for people who have power, as they have had in many British labor unions, to be better informed as they exercise that power. Some panelists, a number of them from ethnic minorities, contended that knowledge alone is not enough. They said that civic education should encourage active, constructive participation in politics and that it should help people understand how to make positive use of power. A few expressed concern over the possibility that the beliefs and values of teachers and personnel employed in agencies other than schools, if publicly expressed, might increase pressure for censorship or other forms of retaliation and restraint.

Because of the nuclear threat and the increasing interdependence of nations, several panelists felt that representatives of all national governments, as they meet on their international frontiers, must more explicitly recognize the danger in aggression. These interview tapes also bore testimony to the importance of negotiation—of compromise, cooperation, cooperative decision making, and the resolution of conflicts. Extrapolating this need downward to the national, state, and local levels within U.S. borders, the development of these same skills of interaction among the young presumably should become a new, vigorous dimension in civic education for the future. Certain panelists even named process skills—which they defined as the ability to work well with other humans—as survival skills to be learned through civic education.

One final point bearing on citizenship experiences can be inferred from the preceding paragraphs. This is the substantial confidence that panelists evidently shared in what schools in particular—among all educational resources—could accomplish to strengthen democracy as well as to brighten our human prospects for the third millennium. An internationally respected panel member, Ralph Tyler, put it this way:

> The place that has the greatest promise of being an ideal democratic society—as I look over everything in our society—is the

school. Even though some schools are troubled by conflicts, mostly begun and pushed by the parents, by and large they are a microcosm of democracy where people care, or are learning to care, about others. In most teachers and students alike, there is a degree of fairness and of justice. Lots of kids participate in the planning and in the outcomes of what they do.

Our efforts to make our society more democratic beyond the schools' walls and playgrounds is going to be aided tremendously by maintaining as we have in this country—and better than in any other country—a school environment in which teachers try to be democratic in their relations with students and with one another.

There are very few teachers who are cruel or who look down upon persons who come from a lower economic group or a different ethnic group. I believe that this important human quality is essential to maintain our pluralistic society. We must preserve this kind of school atmosphere and the values of what John Dewey called "a society in miniature."

WORTHY USE OF LEISURE.   The nature of society some 60 or 70 years ago is reflected in part in comments the Commission on the Reorganization of Secondary Education made on the worthy use of leisure. Reading between the lines of the 1918 document, one senses that work days were long, that arduous physical labor in the United States had yet to be tempered by a widespread use of machines, and that leisure was something pursued either on a religious day of rest or on brief holidays rather than in intervals spread throughout the week.

The work ethic, perhaps a bit incongruously, sometimes infiltrated the 1918 approach to leisure so that it would be used in "worthy" ways. To illustrate, the school was advised to organize recreational activities so "that they will contribute simultaneously to other ends of education" that improve the mind or increase the individual's knowledge.

The NEA panelists identified the changing meaning of "work" and "leisure" in the contemporary U.S. scene as one of ten major developments that are influencing the future. When their thinking was probed specifically with respect to the worthy use of leisure, several additional points arose.

The line dividing work and leisure is beginning to blur, consultants agreed, both because there is more time for relaxation available to more people today and because an energy-intensive as opposed to a labor-intensive economy leaves them less physically fatigued. The breakdown of the work–leisure dichotomy probably will be furthered as more men and women engage in work-type activities that have now begun to assume more of a recreational or re-creative nature. Yard care, redecorating a room, crocheting, gourmet cooking, building a carport—all of these involve work, but they also assume the guise or status of leisure-time activities since they are undertaken outside of the employment time that is spent on the assembly line, at drawing boards, at the cash register, or in the classroom.

Sixty years ago, the Commission on the Reorganization of Secondary Education wrote that leisure was intended to recreate body, mind, and spirit and enrich the personality through experiences involving music, art, literature, drama, and social activity. Today, too, leisure time is well used for re-creative purposes and as a means to self-fulfillment, but the channels education should seek to open, the NEA panelists say, are much broader, and the time for enjoying leisure is potentially greater.

As education seeks to enhance the ability to enjoy free time, it also needs to show awareness of a factor that is sometimes overlooked: the limited leisure of millions of people who are obliged to spend long additional hours toiling on a second job or working overtime because of the gap between their income and their aspirations or needs. Here schools and other educative agencies continue to be challenged to develop the skills and to encourage the productivity that permit the attainment of economic levels at which leisure time is available.

A second, more subtle, factor related to leisure time is that increasing complexity in Americans' lives erodes time that might otherwise be used for re-creative, self-fulfilling activity. The wife and mother or husband and father of 1976 has many gadgets and devices that their parents or grandparents lacked, but also many tasks to perform that were mostly unknown to their grandparents. Among them are taxiing children to school, making simple repairs or finding a plumber with time to repair a dishwasher or a garbage disposal unit, serving as a host or hostess at a dinner for a spouse's clients, standing in line at the supermarket, zipping children's jackets or tying their shoelaces, searching for a slot in which to park, trying to cope with bills to be paid and tax records to be preserved—the list is endless. Furthermore, as noted earlier, by the mid-1970's over half of the mothers of school-age children were holding down a full-time or a part-time job in addition to sharing in home responsibilities. While this factor varies with both sex roles and with economic conditions, it provides a new role for education: helping young and old alike to wrestle with complexity in order to prevent its completely eroding their leisure time.

ETHICAL CHARACTER. "In a democratic society ethical character becomes paramount among the [seven] objectives," the authors of the cardinal principles declared. In 1976, panelists believed that the task of developing ethical character was, if anything, more important during the present era of moral and spiritual crises than it has been in the past. While they made rather few specific suggestions as to what education might do to strengthen or build ethical character, they clearly recognized and defined the seventh cardinal principle as an educational imperative. The following paragraphs attempt to capture the spirit of the statements regarding character which were obtained in the interviews with panelists.

When one contemplates developing ethical character as an educational imperative, it is well to note, as some panelists did, that young and old alike need ethical models—models that leaders often provide, whether they be in government, labor, industry, the church, education, or the world of entertainment. But to have ethical leadership, we must also have a society that honors and supports or elects genuinely good "model" leadership. The process of creating or re-creating an ethical society, therefore, becomes evolutionary and interactive.

The panelists contended that we need a renewal of respect—merited respect—for the institutions that give democracy, the human conscience, and the individual life their meanings. We also need to develop, through group consensus, basic guideposts that will give strength and meaning to social and educational policies. But there is a limit to what leadership in our government and other institutions can accomplish—a point at which democratic *processes* must vitalize policy making and its implementation. Here the individual and his or her possession of ethical standards becomes crucial. Furthermore, it is in devising or developing those experiences that create what we label "ethical character" that the family (or affinity group) and the school, among all educational agencies, are likely to have the greatest influence.

Above all others, these two settings—the family and the school—strengthen or diminish the ability to resist manipulation. They either nurture or undercut the decisiveness needed to respond without confusion to basic choices—the knack of learning to triumph over inner and outer turmoil. Here one either develops the talent for self-direction or learns to accept the dictates of tyrannical machines, or authorities, or of the expert with the answers.

In the aggregate, a number of the NEA tapes suggest—with many voices and accents—that, as they guide young people toward the acquisition of ethical character, parents and teachers need to reassess the importance of a reasoned discipline and of rules that are firm and fair rather than harsh and quixotic. In the process they must keep their awareness that ethical character grows from *within* as wholesome personhood is achieved. It cannot be *imposed,* and the success of love and guidance and discipline is demonstrated as the clear need for external parent-teacher control in early childhood diminishes in the middle school years and becomes negligible in later adolescence.

Furthermore, in any culture, ethical character also calls for an awareness of right and wrong in that culture and for a rejection of a relativism that denies, if only by implication, that there are such things as the common good and the general welfare.

The re-examination of educational goals, however interesting and provocative, is little more than an exercise in futility unless the revisitation of objectives eventuates in some form of action. In view of tomorrow's probable world and in the context of goals that seem reasonable for teachers to pursue during the years that lead toward 2001 A.D., what does one *do?* What are education's "imperative responsibilities" for the next quarter century and how does the teacher approach the tasks that responsibilities imply?

We turn now to the *action* stage of this discussion as we focus on the world as a community, on the quest for peace, on neglected human rights, and on the creation of a more humane society.

CHAPTER V
CARDINAL PREMISES FOR
21ST CENTURY EDUCATION

The United States is not a fatigued society sustained by fading and inaccurate remembrances of past power and leadership. It is a vital culture with a belief in the future and with the will, the imagination, and the energy to clothe this belief in reality. Indeed, in the late 1970's, the country promises to continue to produce the unique brand of skill and wisdom represented by such events as the successful landing of a spacecraft on Mars and by such fads as the entertaining adolescent exuberance of chatter in the argot created by Citizen Band radio buffs.

In the pursuit of better futures—of greater equity and security, improved financial status, better and ecologically benign technologies, and responsible freedom—the U.S. genius for employing education promises to be even more important than it has been during the 200 years since our spin-off from England. There was no dispute among the NEA International Panelists as to the importance of education in the remaining decades of the present century. Less predictable at the outset of the interviews was the general consensus that surfaced with respect to educational premises that should be explored as the country continues its efforts to develop a human needs curriculum that is designed to serve learners of all ages successfully.

The panelists' conceptions of the imperative responsibilities of U.S. education, reflected in 28 premises that often suggest provocative future changes in practice, provide the focal points for this section of the report.

EDUCATION AND SCHOOLING.   In response to the question on imperative skills on which educators ought to focus, one point was made repeatedly; namely, that *education* needed to be seen in a much broader context than the setting in which formal schooling presently occurs. A West Coast engineer and student of the future at the Stanford Research Institute, Willis Harman, came right to the point: "The importance of education is crucial," he said, "but I am less certain of the value of schooling as we face the problems of the next 20 years." Three thousand miles away another panelist, agronomist and world authority on food production Lester Brown, commented in the same vein: "Changes in our attitudes, values, life-styles, and institutions must come quickly. As new priorities and policies develop, the formal education system in our schools may not be able to play as big a role as it heretofore has done."

Each of these persons went on to make two points. According to Harman, as we focus on the immediate social problems *of the next two decades* we need to remember that *children now in school will not be decision-makers for nearly a generation.* As a result, other educational agencies such as books, television, and newspapers must assume greater and more mature responsibility for the continuing instruction of both children and adults.

As Brown saw it, many adults today can discuss at length such topics as pollution and resource depletion, topics which generally were not taught in school 20 or 30 years ago because *their importance at that time usually was not recognized in the curriculum.* These adults had, therefore, obtained most of their current information from educational agencies other than schools.

Lawrence Cremin also urged that any premises or principles for guiding educational change take into consideration "where any given thing that needs to be learned can best be learned," and that "when we decide where to teach it, keep in mind that it may have been taught or is being taught somewhere else, either correctly or incorrectly."

It seems reasonable to infer from testimony provided by the tapes that the panel was not seeking to downgrade the work of U.S. public and independent schools. Rather, it was the general opinion of participants that the pressures of life for the next several decades promised to be such that traditional schooling alone could not be expected to meet the responsibilities which, in all probability, will place heavy demands on *all* educational resources.

PRINCIPLES AND PREMISES.   While it was the NEA's intent to reframe, to update, or to expand the cardinal *principles* of education, readers will quickly note that this section of the report deals with cardinal *premises.* This semantic switch was made for two reasons. First, the original seven principles apparently were intended to be a statement of *goals,* and, as such, they were reexamined in Chapter IV of this report. Second, the premises presented here are statements suggesting how U.S. education, including schooling, might best perform the many tasks that need to be undertaken in the next quarter-century. They are *guides to action* suggested by the panelists, *not goals* such as "vocational competence." Also, in a time of uncertainty, of rapid change, and of complexity it seems prudent to write in terms of *premises,* in terms of ideas to be explored, rather than in terms of *principles,* which have a dictionary meaning of "fundamental truth" or "doctrine."

An examination of the publications produced by UN agencies and task forces suggested that many of the cardinal premises of education for the 21st century probably are applicable in the world community as well as in the United States. Some overseas panelists felt that this would be so. Because of cross-cultural subtleties, however, no claim is made that the premises are intended for export. Nonetheless, it is the hope of the NEA Bicentennial Committee that many of the premises can transcend national boundaries, at least in the more industrialized countries.[1]

CARDINAL PREMISES FOR EDUCATIONAL CHANGE: 1976–2001.   A total of 28 guidelines for educational change were identified in the 46 statements obtained from the NEA's International Panel and from conversations with 95 young people of secondary school age. Since so many ideas were voiced, some organization became necessary for purposes of presentation. As the premises were examined, it became evident that some were *general* ones while others were related to *process.* One cluster was concerned with *structure, with school organization, or with educa-*

---

[1]As François Blanchard of the Syndicat National des Enseignements de Sécond Degré phrased it, "it has become apparent that certain general characteristics are shared in common at least by all those countries that have attained a certain degree of economic development." (Writer's translation of M. Blanchard's statement.)

tional policy, while the fourth and largest group pertained to *content and instruction.* The 28 premises are listed and discussed under these four headings.

GENERAL PREMISES.   While all of the proposals for improving teaching and learning are roughly of coordinate importance, they differ somewhat in focus. The general premises are broad ones and tend to permeate process, organization, and the content of instruction.[2]

I.   The need to develop a spirit of "global community" in an increasingly interdependent world has reaffirmed an important task for education: to recognize and to respect the concepts of multiethnic, polycultural, and multilingual education in pluralistic societies both in the United States and abroad.   A feeling of community, of social cohesion, of shared commitment, and of identity with men and women everywhere is needed on a planet in which there are no longer any far-away places and where people have a mutual need to share ideas, to engage in trade, and to learn to accept and to respect their diversity. In this world, people meet and interact daily on human frontiers that have taken the place of the 19th century's geographical frontiers. In these contacts, mutual respect and good will are essential yet cannot be achieved without insights into cultural pluralism.

II.   Education has assumed new significance as a positive force for peace in a world capable of destroying itself.   Humankind's childhood ended with the first explosion of an atomic weapon. Since such weapons are, for practical purposes, too dangerous to use, education must strive to provide such survival skills as learning to replace force with persuasion, discrimination with equity, narrow nationalism with international perspectives, and authoritarianism with participation. This requires changes in the cli-

---

[2]After reading the 28 premises, one of the original Project Pre-Planning Committee was asked, "Could you rank the premises in importance?" Her response: "That's like asking a centipede to decide which his most important leg is. They're all necessary."

mate or tone of U.S. schools: an increase in warmth, in trust, and in the command of such fundamental process skills as knowing how to develop good, enduring human relations.

III.   Learning is a lifelong process, and education, therefore, should be seen as a seamless continuum of experiences from early childhood to old age.   One begins to learn at birth, and the need for social and intellectual input to make a person effective extends throughout life. Education does not terminate; it merely has terminating phases. Neither is education merely recurrent or periodic; it is ongoing—an *éducation permanent,* according to an overseas panelist. Education is a lifelong process, not a hurdle to be jumped so that diplomas or certificates can be awarded.

IV.   The value to the learners of their experiences obtained through education is more important than the routes they may follow in obtaining those experiences.   Educational processes need to be more flexible, more rich in choices, and less restricted by red tape and fine-print admissions procedures. There is a need to recognize more clearly that much important knowledge is acquired on trails that lead one beyond the confines of the school. Furthermore, what is learned in school can be made more valuable to individual learners if everyone is not expected to follow the same academic road map.

V.   There are standards that are essential to life on a planet sometimes imperiled by the less thoughtful of its human population.   A consensus needs to be reached with respect to secular "commandments" that are an expression of values chosen to serve as referents while humankind works to restore, or to husband, its resources in an overexploited environment.

PREMISES PERTAINING TO PROCESS.[3]   The second group of cardinal premises is based on a phenomenon of which

---

[3]Because of the importance of "process," of ways of working together effectively, the reader is reminded that Chapter VI deals with group processes in program planning and development.

most teachers are aware: it isn't just *what* you do, but also *how* you do it that makes a difference. In other words, the *processes* one follows are likely to determine to a considerable degree the success or failure of a given venture. Opportunities to work closely with others on matters of common concern bring satisfaction through involvement, clarify and refine interpersonal relations, deepen understanding of what is involved in a project, and are consistent with Carl Sandburg's pointed reminder that "*every*body is smarter than *any*body."

VI. The aspirations and abilities of the student are best served when the student's learning experiences are at least partly self-directed rather than selected entirely by teachers. Schooling should reflect a willingness on the part of both teacher and learner to seek together the answers to problems that neither may as yet fully understand.

VII. Because of the impact of the attitudes, comments, and actions of teachers (the "hidden curriculum," reflecting what teachers really value) greater efforts should be made to insure that this latent curriculum becomes clear and provides wholesome input for the learner.[4] The inflections, expressions, and body language of teachers communicate many things, such as their prejudices, displeasure, or satisfaction—what they really feel and truly value. Teachers should reflect positive, constructive values since children learn their life roles more through the *examples* adults set than through the *precepts* and *preachments* they hear.

VIII. Because the experiences of each learner are unique, teachers should expect a wide range of performance from children, youth, and adults. Special heed should be given to policies that govern "success" and "failure" since it is neither psychologically sound nor good academic policy to expect humans to fit the procrustean standards of the normal curve.

---

[4]Chapter IX, in its emphasis on moral education, concerns itself in more depth with the hidden curriculum and the positive and negative learnings that children and youth acquire through it.

IX. Good instruction is personalized rather than individualized. Classical *individualized* instruction was designed to help learners reach or exceed grade-level standards and to perform well on standardized tests. *Personalized* instruction recognizes that children and youth mature at different rates and is designed to help them reach whatever competency level they can reach, but without premature or unreasonable pressures for academic performance. Personalized teaching does not imply a lack of standards; it does recognize that all learners follow unique physical, social, and academic growth patterns.

PREMISES RELATED TO EDUCATIONAL STRUCTURE, ORGANIZATION, OR POLICY. As used here, *structure* refers to school organization such as the K–6–6, K–8–4, K–4–4–4 plans. *Policy* refers to the forms of school practice and governance which are reflected in grouping plans, discipline, report cards, promotion and failure, admission age, and analogous practices.

X. The opportunity for universal early childhood education should be an integral part of the structure of education in a seamless learning continuum. As this premise becomes a reality, at approximately age two, social services, including parent education, would be provided and measures taken to guard against such problems as child battering, abuse, or neglect. Data from tests to verify normal physical, mental, and verbal development also would be sought. Actual attendance in nursery-kindergarten programs probably would not begin until age three or four and would be two to three years in length.[5]

XI. Adult education that exceeds mere literacy should receive worldwide emphasis. The demands placed on the earth's total population during the next several decades will require appreciably more than a low level of functional literacy. Men and women everywhere will need to begin to develop the educated person's

_____

[5]Models of a structure for U.S. education that includes early childhood education and provisions for older learners are suggested in Chapter VIII.

cross-cultural, social, economic, political, and biospheric under-standings. This premise begs for rapid follow-through because the actual number (although not the proportionate number) of adult illiterates since 1960 has increased in some regions due to popula-tion growth, and the "higher literacy" of understandings has suf-fered accordingly.

XII. Continuing educational opportunities should be designed to serve both mature (past 30) and senior (past 60) learners. The necessity that adults keep well informed, the se-quence of different jobs that many workers are beginning to hold, new fields that require new skills, possibilities for postretirement careers, and the prospect—but by no means the certitude—of more leisure time for learning add up to a substantial number of reasons for lifelong education.

XIII. Particularly at the transnational level, the applica-tion of instructional systems and technologies can make im-portant contributions to education as ideas, knowledge, and know-how are shared with the illiterate and the semiliterate in order to further their education. However, the use of systems and of media must be consonant with carefully reasoned human values. Machines are of proven value in performing certain educational tasks; however, they also can help educators to do the wrong things more quickly unless humane values are implemented. Also, there is the ever-present possibility that unscrupulous, police-state leadership will use educational media—including con-trolled schooling—to further their power and ambitions.

XIV. Sharply delineated segments of education based on K–6–6 type grade levels ought to be eliminated as soon as feasible. Ability, motivation, and readiness rather than certificates or di-plomas should serve as the learner's prime credentials. However much teachers may strive to control them, the develop-mental pathway followed by each individual defies the normal curve. Personal, social, and academic growth simply do not move ahead on an even front nor follow a set schedule. The policy of chopping the continuum of learning into segments in which learners arbitrarily are grouped has lost the purpose it served a century ago and also is not in touch with the realities of the lifelong education needed today.

XV.   When and where teaching and learning occur must not be bounded either by the school's walls or by our preconceived ideas as to what should be learned at the once-traditional age for learning it.   There are many curriculums in home, school, factory, military forces, church, in a wide variety of comparable social agencies, and on the streets of the city and village. Schools should be increasingly aware of and more carefully study and coordinate efforts with these "concomitant curriculums" since all are likely to flourish in the 1980's and 1990's. More children and youth should be encouraged to seek to engage in socially useful service learning and apprentice experiences as schools capitalize on the curricula of other social agencies.[6]

XVI.   Persons in the field of career or occupational education should develop their programs in ways which recognize even more fully that vocational activity—the jobs held and services performed—often is sequential and will require greater versatility from members of the work force in the years ahead.   Under such circumstances the personal-social adjustments that mobility requires should receive attention from educators along with necessary multiprofessional skills and the continuing education that they seem likely to require.

XVII.   Traditional patterns of home–school relations need to be reconsidered and perhaps sharply modified in recognition of changes in the family which, in many instances today, is often an "affinity group" rather than the nuclear family consisting of mother, father, and children.   In many rural areas and in cities both large and small, fewer than half of the families resemble the 1930 model in which Dick and Jane, Baby and their pets grew up.

---

[6]Chapters VIII and IX attempt to suggest how schools may be reorganized to foster out-of-school learning and to cope with urban problems.

PREMISES WITH A BEARING ON CONTENT AND INSTRUCTION. *Content,* in the premises that follow, refers to the substance of experiences designed to help the learner control and contribute to her/his environment for worthy purposes. *Instruction* is defined as those strategies that facilitate or serve as a lubricant for the processes involved in teaching and in learning.

XVIII. *Present social trends, which are characterized by accelerating change and increasing complexity, have enhanced the need for basic communication skills such as the ability to handle the written and spoken word and to deal with number concepts.* Great improvements in educational technology such as the use of computers and increasingly effective software for individually guided instruction have not reduced but have increased the need to read with understanding, to work accurately with number concepts, and to speak one's language without ambiguity and with an understanding of the ways in which messages influence the attitudes and mediate the behavior of others.

XIX. *Valid methods of instruction vary from one learner to another, hence the goal of equitable educational opportunity can be approached only when schooling provides—at least in some respects—experiences that are different for each student.* Furthermore, since each student is different, each will have different experiences regardless of what his school provides—yet most learning experiences continue to be planned for the mythical average child. Actually, rapid learners should be challenged by work that is demanding and interesting. Slower learners should be spared from the pressures created by requirements that are unreasonable for *them.* All normal learners should be expected to reach a point where they are useful both to themselves and to society. To serve this end, *problem-preventing* education that begins in early childhood is vastly superior to *compensatory* education provided at a later time in life.

XX. *Traditional instructional methods should be expanded to include problem-solving approaches, and their emphasis on cognition and on valuing should be renewed.* In a stressful, transitional world, there is danger in moving from a problem to a hasty solution. Learners of all ages need to acquire the commonsense habit of thinking and valuing before making decisions.

XXI.   Interdisciplinary learning should be stressed and the art of comprehending and anticipating complex relationships should be fostered.   Fields of knowledge rapidly are becoming more closely associated, and interdisciplinary solutions to problems are increasingly common. It follows that skills for coping with complex interrelationships, including their human components, need to be acquired.

XXII.   Good vocational or occupational education should be more thoroughly permeated by the content of a general or "liberalizing" education; conversely, it should be recognized that a sound liberal education also will be inherently vocational in the years ahead.   The mobility of workers, the diverse positions they may hold, recreational and leisure-time activities, and the need for broadly educated citizens combine to suggest that the general education component in occupational education will increase.

XXIII.   Because human differences and educational uniformity cannot be reconciled, the testing and measurement of content skills should be evaluated on an individual basis.   Academic and social assessments, furthermore, should be so conducted that emphasis is placed on *how* learning experiences are influencing the students' behavior as well as on their attainments. Evaluation also must be continuous because, to some degree, every learner is a different person each morning as a result of the new social and intellectual input that was acquired the day or night before.

XIV.   There is a need to teach the concept of alternative futures since, lacking a desirable image of tomorrow's possible worlds, one lacks purpose, goals, and the motivating spirit of community that are needed to serve as guides to action.   The future can become any one out of many possible futures, depending on human behavior. The next 10 to 20 years are crucial ones because social decisions during this interval will substantially determine whether the 21st century is to be a retrogressive era or a rewarding time in which to be alive. Educational agencies other than schools have particular responsibility for preparing adults to give definite form to their image of a desirable future as well as the personal and social motivation to strive for it.

XXV.   Instruction in subject matter fields should develop a deepening understanding of contemporary threats to the biosphere, include socially useful service in its maintenance, and communicate to youth the need for achieving balance or equilibrium between humans and their environment.   To give meaning to this premise, instruction and content should be designed to develop the will, the expertise, and the skills that are needed if people are to make greater progress in attacking such universal problems as hunger, regional overpopulation, diminishing resources, increasing debt, and maldistribution of goods.

XXVI.   So that desirable alternative futures can be envisioned, work in the social studies should be redesigned so as to promote a grasp of human geography and of planetary cultures as they exist today.   Old and young alike, through all available forms of education, need to know more about what is going on in every quarter of the globe; the meaning of explosive political, economic, and military struggles; how people see themselves; and how they feel toward others. The past must become more than fables masquerading as history; problems of the present, such as resource depletion, must be faced frankly; the future ought to be methodically studied through carefully projected scenarios that suggest both the planning for 2050 that needs to be done and the guidelines we can use now in the 1976–2001 interval.

XXVII.   In studying possible futures the natural and physical sciences, both in content and methodology, should serve as illustrations of truth-validating inquiry.   Without downgrading the importance of the sciences as systematized knowledge, it is important to keep in mind that many students will not be professional scientists and that scientific knowledge now ages quickly. Young learners can, however, make lifelong use of the methods of science as a way of thinking, inquiring, and acting.

XXVIII.   In the symbolic sciences—language arts, foreign language, mathematics, linguistics, and the like—more heed should be given both to basic communication skills as well as to the ability to recognize propaganda, shoddy advertising, and political doubletalk.   As the means and the volume of communication have improved in the last 20 or 30 years, clarity in the meaning of what is communicated probably has declined. Education needs to stress the art of communicating ideas clearly and how to analyze and enjoy what is seen, heard, and read in a world rich in the symbols of language.

PREMISES THAT WERE STRESSED BY YOUTH. [7]   The secondary school panel of youth selected for participation in the NEA project was not asked explicitly to identify cardinal premises to guide education for the next 25 years. Instead the 95 young respondents simply were asked what they thought might be done to improve their schools and their schooling.

Although their thoughts were phrased in many different ways, three points came through clearly. First, in a world that youth find frustrating, distressing, and sometimes frightening, the need for *coping* skills and techniques was expressed. Made uneasy by the widespread malaise and troubles of the present—the profound global turmoil of which the media constantly reminded them—the students clearly recognized the importance of good guidance and better preparation in their schooling so that they could live good and useful lives in a world of inter- and intra-dependence.

A second quality that youth sought in its schools is more difficult to capture in words. The young people wanted schools that *cared* about them. The tapes sometimes poignantly revealed loneliness. The image of the "good" teacher was not merely one who was bright, good-looking, or well informed. It was a person who

---

[7]Excerpts from the youth tapes published in the September 1976 issue of *Phi Delta Kappan* are included in Appendix B.

radiated warmth and genuine interest in students. Parents who sub-
stituted things rather than giving of their time and of themselves,
parents who didn't seem to care, and absentee parents also troubled
many boys and girls. Some spoke of having no one other than their
peer group for companionship and of no place other than the
streets for a "home."

Finally, the young sought help in *communicating.* They were not
speaking here of better language instruction or of forensic skills,
but of the opportunity to have someone to talk with, someone to
whom they could listen, someone to whom and with whom they
could communicate and share their feelings, hopes, and concerns.

Reduced to their basic meanings, the comments made by youth
indicate that they hope for schools characterized by a climate of
love and of understanding that will build the inner security that the
troubled present and an uncertain future require. *Coping, caring,
communicating: the three words suggest a premise charged with emotion.
The schools youth seek are schools that provide coping skills for facing a
world that is often harsh and sometimes frightening; schools that are
warmly humane because teachers care; and schools that give an opportunity to communicate inner feelings without fear of ridicule or re-
prisal.* This is easy to say, but truly difficult to realize in practice.

SUMMARY.   A careful reading of the 28 premises suggests
that the panelists had a great deal of confidence in what education
in the United States can accomplish. The premises also imply that a
great deal also remains to be accomplished in the schools. Many of
the needed reforms already have been proposed by the NEA or
discussed during the years past in *Today's Education.* An important
point is the *accelerated* rate of change in educational practices that
the premises encourage.

Five key concepts.   While the 28 premises cover a great deal of
territory, most of them, if they are to be carried out, would appear
to involve creating and strengthening five abilities or capacities in
learners. One of these is an in-depth knowledge of the world and
its peoples; a knowledge of *realities.* A second strategy for schools
to apply is developing awareness of *alternative solutions* to problems, a requisite in a world in which compromise and persuasion

must replace force. Developing sensitivity to the *consequences* of one's choices is a third ability to be sought, along with a closely related fourth skill: cultivation of the insights and values that support wise *choices* among alternatives. Finally, a good education should provide the skills, the information, and the motivation that are requisites for *implementation*. This includes (*a*) knowledge of the processes that are effective when people work together, (*b*) knowledge of the structure or organizational procedures that help people to carry out their ideas and plans, and (*c*) command of both content and the sources of content which help insure that informed action is taken on a project.

A knowledge of realities, of alternative solutions and their consequences, the ability to choose wisely and to carry out ideas—these talents, acquired from warm and understanding teachers, seem to capture the spirit of the premises of both the adult and youth panelists.

From premises to policies.   The reinterpretations of the seven cardinal principles and the 28 premises extracted from the NEA tapes will, at best, be a conversation piece or footnote to educational history (or at worst an exercise in futility) unless the Association through its members and the thousands of communities in which they work continue to strive for educational reforms such as the principles and the premises suggest.

As Consuelo Nieto put it, "The NEA must be more than a union [concerned with] more than salary and working conditions. The Association must provide teachers with resources for dealing with students' needs." Furthermore, the NEA in its own pronouncements should be dedicated to "pursuing a series of programs to prepare for major reform in education."[8]

It is with the transition from educational principles and premises to emerging educational policies and improved practices that the next four chapters concern themselves.

---

[8]*NEA Bicentennial Ideabook.* Washington, D.C.: the Association, 1975. p. 8.

CHAPTER VI
WORKING TOGETHER FOR
CURRICULUM REFORM

Over a quarter of a century ago, historian Henry Steele Commager,[1] in a classic statement for its era, identified four important contributions made by the public and independent schools of the United States. They have, he said, helped make self-government work by providing a literate citizenry, by creating national unity despite strong disruptive forces, by Americanizing persons immigrating to what probably is the most polyglot of modern nations, and by enabling this diverse society to stand strong and free without either ruinous political ruptures or riotous economic and social privilege.

EDUCATIONAL LEADERSHIP: YESTERDAY. The leadership that led to the contributions which Commager identified has deep roots in our history and has found expression, for example, in the voices of such gifted, influential, and determined people as Thomas Jefferson, Horace Mann, Elizabeth Peabody, Henry Barnard, and Susan Blow. In the past, much leadership in education stemmed from a single, forceful personality. The attributes of such a person frequently were (a) great breadth and grasp of information, (b) strong opinions, (c) self-confidence, (d) skill in communicating ideas, and (e) a willingness to do the hard work that responsibility usually brings with it.

While forceful leadership and personal attributes, such as those listed, remain desirable in our time, the *role* of leadership in educa-

---

[1]Henry Steele Commager, "Our Schools Have Kept Us Free," *Life* 29:46–47; October 16, 1950.

tional planning and implementing has changed significantly since 1950 and particularly since 1965. Not only in education but in government, in industry, and in business there has been a growing skepticism with regard to the traditional concept of the authoritarian leader and of directive leadership.

Criticisms of old-style "Napoleonic" leadership include:

1. The way in which the Great Leader weakens her/his followers by their growing belief in her/his omniscience
2. The Great Leader's loss of perspective and judgment as she/he becomes surrounded by associates who are either incapable of or afraid of offering criticism when making suggestions
3. The Great Leader's inability to tolerate seeming or potential rivals—even loyal followers—because of the real or fancied threats they pose.

Small wonder that so many personal empires—financial or political—tend to wobble and then to collapse after a Great Leader's death or defeat, and sometimes even sooner.

EDUCATIONAL LEADERSHIP: TODAY AND TOMORROW. Not only because of problems and shortcomings in authoritarian leadership but also because of the continuous re-examination of democratic values and processes, concepts of leadership have changed appreciably in recent years. As the schools encounter new opportunities for service and undertake new tasks suggested by the 28 cardinal premises, it seems inevitable that different concepts of leadership will appear and that these concepts will be based on greater participation by more people, thus enabling persons affected by alternative choices and decisions to have a greater share in making them.

Lacking the "collective intelligence" which can be extracted from cooperative planning—from the sharing of ideas and from the consensus that results when good ideas (in a reversal of Gresham's Law) drive out bad ones—U.S. educational planning is likely to flounder from failure to frustration—not unlike Coronado in his futile quest for cities of gold in the American Southwest. The urgency of our educational problems and the limited time in which to develop antidotes to viruses such as the frustration of inner-city children, norm-referenced test scores as major determinants of individual success, and the herding of young people onto intellectual feedlots where all are expected to flourish on the same fodder, simply do not allow teachers the luxury of floundering. The important alternative open to us is developing the *process* skills of group leadership.

THE "GROUP PROCESS" APPROACH TO LEADERSHIP. The idea that leadership can reside in a group rather than a Great Leader was expressed 40-odd years ago by Paul Pigors in his classic book, *Leadership or Dominination.* He defined group leadership as "a process of mutual stimulation which, by the successful interplay of relevant individual differences, controls human energy in pursuit of a common cause."[2] In this context, leadership is a *function* which is passed around within a group and which is exercised for a given period of time by anyone who is qualified at this given time to contribute to an attack on a common problem, to meet a group need, or to stretch the imagination and vision of associates.

Put it this way. As teachers, parents, students or others work together to bring about curriculum change, a leader is one who successfully contributes to group thinking and planning so that in the end everyone, or virtually everyone, is pleased or at least reasonably satisfied with the outcome. This is the *leadership of the merit of ideas* in attaining shared goals *rather than the leadership of status.* When group processes are functioning, suggestions or proposals that pass currency in the free market of ideas have a full and fair chance to determine what decisions shall be made and what action shall be taken. Defensible *values* and persuasive, sound *ideas* rather than position or rank are what matter.

SOME VALUES OF COOPERATIVE GROUP PROCESSES IN CURRICULUM CHANGE. As teachers and other members of the community (including young people!) work together to reform and improve education, they will discover a number of virtues in the *process* of working together. Some of the clearly

---

[2]Paul Pigors, *Leadership or Domination.* New York: Houghton, Mifflin Co. 1935. p. 16.

demonstrable values of cooperative group action include the following:

1. Public understanding and public relations will be improved because the citizens and teachers who participate can explain to others in the community more clearly and explicitly (a) the decisions reached, (b) why they were reached, and (c) how they promise better to serve educational needs through the proposed reforms.

2. The morale of a group is greatly improved when each participant feels that her/his ideas are welcome and, if they have sufficient merit, that they will influence outcomes.

3. Through group processes and participation the odds are likely to favor the achievement of a more complete inventory of possible approaches to school programs through desirable innovations such as are suggested by the 28 premises.

4. There is a clearer understanding of proposed policies for curriculum improvement, and these policies are developed with greater initiative and sympathy when teacher and community share in reaching the decisions which support them.

5. The individual becomes more knowledgeable through participation since this participation improves understanding of both the theory and the application of democracy.

6. The community and the teacher generally support more strongly those educational policies and practices which they have examined and recommended as distinct from those put into operation by administrative edict.

7. How teachers work with children and youth is shaped by their experiences; therefore, teachers are more likely to work with students in a democratic fashion when they themselves have engaged in the group processes of cooperative thinking, planning, and executing curriculum policies.

CAUTIONS TO OBSERVE WHEN ENGAGING IN GROUP PROCESSES. While a strong case can be made for group processes as a basis for curriculum planning that anticipates educational needs between the 1970's and the year 2001, the experiences of participants in cooperative planning quickly make clear that a "process approach" requires maturity and skill in human relations plus the courage required by old-fashioned, gutsy give-and-take.

Some of the pitfalls in "process" to be avoided are obvious ones. Others are more subtle. Three obvious potential difficulties are related to *time,* *"homework,"* and *follow-up.* Cooperative action does require a major investment of one's time—a precious commodity in the crowded days of many Americans. Ample time must be budgeted in advance; for the privilege of participating in decisions, teachers and other community members must invest many hours that might otherwise be spent with one's family, working on preparation for the next day in the classroom, or relaxing with a good book or on the golf course. Frustration mounts quickly if one is not psychologically prepared to rebudget his or her time.

Closely related to the time problem is the "homework" that is a prerequisite to participation in cooperative curriculum planning. Participants need to bone up on the issues and topics under discussion. If they fail to do so, group thinking becomes little more than a pooling of ignorance and, again, frustration mounts. Follow-up problems is a euphemism for the dirty work that someone has to do—to perform the tasks and engage in the toil of record-keeping, telephoning reminders to insure attendance, typing and mimeographing, and so on, that are a part of group discussion meetings.

A more subtle problem, when groups convene to think and plan, is two-edged: (a) how to avoid being dominated by a small part of the group, and (b) how to protect minority opinion from being overwhelmed or dominated by the majority of a given group. While majority decisions are essential in American democracy, as every presidential election illustrates, in the community planning of educational reforms it is psychologically important to eliminate as much disagreement as possible. This involves time and patience. It also places a premium on mature behavior. One of the most valuable of group process skills is the ability of participants to recognize the need for many points of view to be recognized—and also to sense that the group grows restless and frustrated when a minority's defensive actions or delaying tactics prolong a decision that a majority seeks to reach.

When group action is stalled or decisions are impeded, the difficulty is sometimes compounded by (a) the problem of "who speaks for whom" as discussions proceed, (b) the challenge of how to cope with participants who have unmet personal needs or other psychological problems and who complicate group interaction because of their hang-ups, and (c) the need to find ways of dealing with persons who have "hidden agendas"—that is, persons who seek to exploit or direct the course of a meeting and regulate the activities of others for purposes of their own choosing. When one of these developments occurs, then there is, indeed, a need for what was mentioned earlier: a good measure of courage so that others in the group can contain the potential harm to cooperative action which problem participants can cause.

The rebel is one more example of the need for the hard-nosed control of cooperative practices by responsible group participants. Rebels are those persons who reject group proposals that displease them. While such individuals tend to discredit themselves by their intransigence, it is nonetheless important to anticipate their feelings and, when possible, cool down rebels who propose to take their marbles and leave the game because they aren't winning.

One additional consideration sometimes arises when group processes are employed in approaches to educational change. This is the authority/responsibility dilemma. The local board of education, with powers delegated by state laws, has certain responsibilities which it literally cannot relinquish. Likewise, administrators are charged with certain functions for which they have responsibility. While an administrator can delegate the *authority* to cooperative planning groups, legally he or she retains the *responsibility* for actions taken and for their outcomes. This creates the authority/responsibility dilemma which those who share in the processes of curriculum reform need to recognize with sympathy, maturity, and understanding. Administrators and boards of education should not be put on a spot with respect, say, to state law by the action proposed by school-community planning groups.

SOME PERSONAL ATTRIBUTES OF THE ABLE PARTICIPANT IN COOPERATIVE CURRICULUM CHANGE. An effective, mature person who is learning to work with others to attain the reforms implied by the 28 cardinal premises is, in the simplest terms, a basically worthy member of the human community. This description is meaningless, however, without a few interpretative paragraphs.

Such persons presumably understand the importance of group processes, decisions, and action. They keep informed with regard to social, economic, and political trends that are shaping the next several decades and participate in appropriate adult activities. They are intellectually curious and alert as well as emotionally secure. They possess a positive and practical democratic philosophy which colors their relationships with others, and they understand at least some of the drives and aspirations that tend to influence the behavior of others. Their own behavior reflects honesty, sincerity, and the courage that candor and integrity require, and they make a continuing effort to improve their general culture.

Our worthy humans, furthermore, are sensitive to the problems of resource depletion, hunger, pollution, and the like. Therefore, their personal activities and recreation are ecologically sound. Their image of good education mirrors their understanding "that the children and youth who will be living in 2050 are just as precious as our own. . . .Because they are, they deserve the best of our time and energy *now* so that 75 years hence they will be better beings because of what we have had the wisdom and the foresight to do."[3]

SUMMARY.   The skills of working together are not easy ones to come by. Also, while there *is* time to begin more effectively to prepare learners of all ages for life in a new millennium, the reformation that U.S. education demands can only come about through a major effort—and this won't be easy either. As the writer has said elsewhere, "our present *vita* is so *dolce* for many persons . . . that they dread any moves that are likely to lessen their present advantages."[4]

But the probable world described in Chapter II—as the NEA panel envisioned it—leaves little choice. New cardinal premises— or locally devised variations—are in need of implementation in our schools, and teachers, students, parents, *all* citizens need to decipher, in their own way and for their own schools, how schooling and education can be recast in ways that more effectively serve the general welfare of their clients.

Meaningful and enduring improvements cannot be imposed because each school is unique and the premises chosen as guides to change are likewise unique to situations. The group process approach to cooperative planning in U.S. schools is important because each community district and each school in each district is unique.

---

[3]Robert J. Havighurst, transcribed from the 1976 NEA panelist tapes.
[4]In the First Annual Robert J. Havighurst Lecture, The University of Chicago, October 1, 1976.

CHAPTER VII
PLANNING CURRICULUM CHANGE
FOR A NEW ERA

With the passage of time, as Chapter IV suggested, the seven cardinal principles of education have become endowed with expanded meanings. The passing years also have produced a number of new or reaffirmed guidelines, as suggested by the 28 cardinal premises. This brings up the interesting and practical question, What curriculum change and innovation do these premises suggest?

In the belief that it will encourage parents and teachers to discuss possible curriculum changes that deal realistically with their unique local community needs and problems, this chapter attempts to look more closely at the cardinal premises and at what they suggest for actual classroom practice. First, however, let us look at some assumptions about curriculum planning, then identify and discuss briefly some of the changes and trends in U.S. life that seem likely to influence education. Then we will take up certain curriculum changes that the 28 premises suggest.

SOME ASSUMPTIONS ABOUT PLANNING CURRICULUM CHANGE. There are six assumptions—perhaps they might better be labeled convictions—about curriculum change that underlie the discussion which follows:

1. The 28 cardinal premises provide reliable guidelines for curriculum development just as the seven cardinal principles, as reinterpreted, continue to provide valid goals.
2. Curriculum planning should be carried forward by parents and teachers working cooperatively in each unique local school unit. Since schools differ one from another, differences should exist among their curriculum plans and their instructional policies.

3. In general terms, we can anticipate probable future developments—both the problems and the opportunities that lie ahead for humanity.[1] Also, we can draw inferences as to what the years ahead will require of educated men and women.

4. Education should be designed for persons of all ages in anticipation of what these humans will need to know and be able to do to survive in the future.

5. Schools are not ineffectual despite occasional raucous criticisms and despite a smattering of faulty educational theory and scattered dismal and unproductive classrooms. These schools do not need to be scrapped and replaced by "deschooled" forms of teaching and learning; rather than alternatives *to* schools we need more alternatives *in* schools.[2]

6. Needed reforms, including those to be made in educational agencies other than schools, in the 1980's and perhaps in the 1990's will not radically alter the instructional environments they now provide. Rather, "reform" will involve the implementation of many of the proposals, ideas, and trends that are already in existence in a limited number of innovative schools.

CHANGES AND TRENDS WITH A BEARING ON U.S. EDUCATION. Although participants on the NEA's International Panel shared their images of the world of 1996 to 2001, a number of forces or developments already making themselves felt in American life also need to be reviewed because of their present or potential impact on education. Teachers and parents will want to keep them in mind when discussing any changes such as those suggested by the 28 cardinal premises. Let us examine a few of the many influences that promise to temper curriculum development for years to come.

---

[1]As Frank McHale has pointed out, the future of the future resides in the present—in what we believe and do *now*. (See *The Future of the Future.* New York: George Braziller Co., 1969).

[2]Typical of the drum-fire of criticism is a ten-part nationally syndicated feature published in 1976. Under the headline, "Johnny Still Can't Read," instruction in reading was called "a national disgrace" and parents were advised to teach their children to read at home if they wanted "to overcome the reading deficiencies produced by the present 'look-say' system of teaching. . . ." (See *The Indianapolis Star,* August 26, 1976, p. 1.)

1. Uncertainty. Some things that are in store for us in the next 20 to 25 years are fairly definite. We will, for example, have less and less oil, as the NEA panelists pointed out. Pollution will create problems for developing nations as they become industrialized, and population problems seem certain to increase before they diminish. But by and large, there is much uncertainty in the world of tomorrow. This suggests that curriculum planning should remain flexible and avoid lock-ins whenever possible.[3] Clear decisions must be reached before action is taken, and uncertainty should not become a pretext for avoiding or postponing them. However, education planning should allow for the unpredictable.

2. Zero population growth. Now familiarly referred to as ZPG, the recent dropoff in the U.S. birth rate is a development that will have a bearing on education for decades.[4] Some considerations posed by ZPG are related to class size, possible higher per-pupil costs as enrollments decline while costs remain high, adapting secondary and postsecondary education to smaller youth cohorts in the 1980's, possible cutbacks in teacher college enrollments, an increase in the number of teachers who are available for positions in educational agencies other than schools, and the prospect of reductions in state funding due to the dropoff in average daily attendance or enrollment.

3. Widening interest in early childhood education. The merits of making early childhood education (ECE) an integral part of both public and independent school programs has been tacitly or explicitly acknowledged by substantial state and federal support programs. Also, for over a century ECE has been warmly advocated by theorists, practitioners, and many parents. Particularly in view of ZPG, programs for young children seem likely to grow in both

---

[3]During a dinner conversation with Kenneth E. Boulding, distinguished economist and social analyst, the writer asked if *anything* definite could be predicted about the future. "One thing is certain," he said with a chuckle. "We can be prepared to be surprised. The only surprise-free future is in the imaginary world we conjure up when we make linear projections."

[4]Zero population growth also serves as an example of uncertainty and unpredictability. Demographers had not anticipated ZPG for at least another 10 to 20 years!

scope and sophistication. Space and well-prepared personnel have become available, too, due to declining elementary school enrollments.

4. Continuation of urban problems. As one of the NEA Pre-Planning Committee members[5] noted:

> The big city has been overtaken by new realities. The history of this country is being shaped in no small degree by what is taking place in these big cities. Their ultimate purpose is to provide and sustain a total living environment that has diversity, that allows freedom of choice, that generates rational interaction among people and between them and their surroundings, and that gives people reasonable opportunities to reach the purposes they seek.
>
> The city is not a mere physical entity composed of buildings, streets, business places, industries, institutions, and government. The city is people—all people: the strong and the weak, the rich and the poor, the newcomer and the old-timer—not living in isolation but interacting, intermingling, cooperating, and competing as they follow diverse pathways and form different social patterns in seeking their ultimate destinies.
>
> Now a tremendous weight of the past must be sloughed off—the concept that the purpose of the school is to *adjust* the child to the "realities" of his existence. . . . No educator with high ideals can ask his pupils to "adjust" to slum living. Slums must be wiped out. We must strive to make urban life more rewarding and satisfying through social decisions and educational changes.

Plainly, the forceful impact of urban life on millions of children and youths will continue to require the skill, the patience, the understanding, and the staunch support of adults who share in curriculum planning.

5. An increase in the number of mature and senior learners.[6] A seemingly inevitable development intimately related to most of

---

[5]William J. Ellena, Superintendent of Schools, the Charlottesville, Virginia, Public Schools, in a letter to the writer dated May 18, 1976.

[6]As used in this report, "mature learners" are drop-ins, aged from 30 to 60 years, in continuing education programs. "Senior learners" are persons over 60 who are engaged in such programs.

American education is the fashion in which the proportion of older citizens will increase. During the next 25 years the median age of our citizens will climb from 28.6 to 34.8 years. In the same time interval, 1975–2000, the number of persons who are 65 or older will escalate from 22 million to 31 million—a jump of almost 50 percent.[7]

The influence of these age shifts on politics, entertainment, housing, education, retail sales, and other dimensions of life in the United States seems difficult to exaggerate. Insofar as education is concerned, the effect is already being felt. In a recent 24-month period the number of people over 35 who enrolled in postsecondary programs increased by 30 percent.[8] During the same period a postsecondary senior learners program in Minneapolis drew four times the anticipated enrollment for short courses on topics such as "How To Live on Social Security Benefits" and "Sex After 60."

Not only may educational agencies have more aged clients, able-bodied sexagenarians could provide a resource if invited to work in the numerous capacities in which they could be used: from kindergartens to colleges, in libraries, hospitals, or YMCA-YWCA programs. A large plurality of active 60- to 75-year-olds, perhaps a majority, undoubtedly would enjoy being of use to themselves and to others in such roles.

6. Behavior modification practices. For over a decade there has been a great deal of interest in psychological, chemical, and electronic approaches to directed behavior.[9] More recently the need for caution has been stressed because, as a French biochemist put it, we are in the position of having acquired some of the power attributed to the ancient gods before we have developed the wisdom to use it.

Also, as psychiatrist John Lion[10] pointed out in *Today's Education,* there is the danger that school workers might make faulty

---

[7]Data cited are from NEA panelist Roy Amara, who based his estimates on U.S. Census Bureau projections.

[8]The 1974–75 recession, the substantial unemployment rate, and sharper competition for jobs no doubt increased the mature learners' decision to return to school.

[9]See, for instance, "Forecast for the 70's," *Today's Education* 58:29–32; January 1969.

[10]"Coping with Violence," *Today's Education* 63:81–85; October 1974.

diagnoses and decisions as to the causes of a given child's disabilities. Obliquely, this potential problem suggests that as teachers and parents contemplate program changes in the schools they might keep in mind Dr. Lion's point that the behavior problems for which chemical therapy has been tried result from faulty school programs rather than from "problem children."[11]

7. *The need for survival skills.* This point needs very little elaboration since the NEA panelists[12] repeatedly made it: in a world grown capable of its own destruction, the ability to attain fair compromises, to mediate, to reach consensus, to understand cultural differences, and so forth, have now become equally as important as a grasp of the nine areas of knowledge which schools seek to develop.[13]

8. *Changing vocational patterns.* Patently, local planning of curriculum change should consider the new meanings that are attaching themselves to the fourth cardinal principle, vocational competence. Changes in the nature of work as well as in the composition of the work force make this highly important.[14]

9. *Changes in the work week of adults.* During the past 30 or 40 years there have been appreciable changes in U.S. work patterns. The work week is shorter, the mobility of the worker is greater, vacations are no longer confined to the summer but are spread throughout the year, and if machines have dehumanized the role of the worker they also have defatigued it and opened new occupational avenues to women in manufacturing or mining, in addition to the clerical, business, and professional positions they held in years past. Finally, many persons work in a variety of jobs—in a chain series of vocational opportunities—that may be as unrelated as the work of hospital orderly and truck driver. U.S. education

---

[11]*Ibid.*, p. 85.

[12]The reader is reminded that many of the points made by panelists have been preserved in the Appendix.

[13]The nine areas of knowledge are reviewed in Chapter VIII.

[14]Changing requirements for vocational education are discussed in Chapters IV and V.

sometimes continues to reflect the pattern of America's agrarian years and should quickly begin to accommodate itself to an era in which only 7 percent of the population is engaged in farming.

10. Increasing teacher power and changing parental aspirations. By 1976, as Marshall Donley has pointed out, "American teachers . . . were relatively well paid, had good job security and benefits, believed in organized effort, and were playing a greater role in their professional and civic lives. No one," Donley adds, "who has observed the history of teacher militancy can expect its future to be less dynamic than its past."[15]

At the same time, parents have become more powerful, articulate, and involved in local control. In curriculum planning, their aspirations, reflected in the education they seek for their children, may not always coincide with those of the teachers with whom they are working. Enduring changes in curricular and administrative structures will need to embody the compromises reached in an atmosphere of mutual respect. The alternative seems likely to be a revolution of rising frustrations rather than a reformation in education.

11. Rising levels of consciousness. Beginning with a few small ripples in the early years of the century, the phenomenon now known as a "heightening of consciousness" began to reach tidal wave proportions by the mid-1960's. Interest in protecting the biosphere from pollution increased. Human rights legislation began to flow like a thousand spring freshets, and domestic opposition to U.S. involvement in Southeast Asia ended our most frustrating war. The status of women, the elderly, the homosexual, ethnic groups, children, and other subsets in the culture was markedly improved. Progress also was made on the task of putting our institutional house in order through investigation and cleanup of such scandals as the Watergate burglary and coverup, multinational corporations, influence-buying, the illegal surveillance activities of the FBI and the CIA, murderous quarreling within Big

---

[15]Marshall O. Donley, Jr., "The American School Teacher: From Obedient Servant to Militant Professional," *Phi Delta Kappan* 58:117; September 1976.

Labor, and abuses that threatened the consumer with food additives, unfair prices, or misleading advertising.

Curriculum planning by parents and teachers and subsequent changes in the classroom that occur as a consequence should deliberately take into account the growing concern for the enhancement of our moral strength and the humaneness which should flourish along with it.

12. Neoconservatism. Somewhat paradoxically, in the 1970's there also has been a trend toward a new conservatism that, at the operational level, sometimes comes into conflict with rising levels of consciousness. This conservatism makes itself felt in politics, in criticisms of education, and in pressure for hard-line policies in the realm of international relations. As Robert Nesbit points out in *The Twilight of Authority,* we are witnessing "rising opposition to the central values of the political community as we have known them for the better part of two centuries: freedom, rights, due process, privacy, and welfare."[16]

Changes in curriculum content and structure inevitably will be influenced not only by trends but by countertrends such as the one mentioned here. The inference to be made when engaging in curriculum development is plain: among the parents, teachers, and other citizens involved there are almost certain to be participants representing both neoconservative and liberal viewpoints. Careful attention must be given by leadership to ways of avoiding conflicts and to tactics for defusing and then reconciling the tensions that inevitably are generated.

13. The recent reappraisal of values in U.S. culture. Roy Amara has pointed out that certain values in U.S. culture are declining.[17] Among them he identified:

   a. The concept that "growth is good" without thought for the consequences to the biosphere

---

[16]Cited by R. Freeman Butts, "Once Again the Question for Liberal Public Educators: Whose Twilight?" *Phi Delta Kappan* 58:6; September 1976.

[17]Dr. Amara made these comments at a meeting of the Washington Association of School Administrators in Olympia on June 16, 1976.

b. The conviction that the application of technology can provide a *deus ex machina* or automatic solution to all problems
c. The dogma that increasing size and centralization means greater efficiency
d. The belief that humanity exists outside nature rather than in a symbiotic or mutually supportive relationship with the ecosphere.

These changing values (and Amara cited evidence to support his conclusions) should have major implications for the 25-year period with which this report is concerned. They bear on both curriculum content and on the hidden curriculum[18] discussed in Chapter IX.

As efforts are made more vigorously to conserve natural and human resources and to attain the selective growth recommended in the second Club of Rome report[19] (a course of action that seems eminently sensible), the effect on our present industrial society could be far-reaching. The control of growth in order to conserve resources and restrict further pollution in our nation will be even more portentous for the industrialized countries if the earth's developing nations succeed in increasing their proportion of the world GNP from 7 to 25 percent, as nations such as Iran plan to do by 2001.[20]

14. Increasing debt and future financial obligations. Although figures are deceptive and open to varied interpretations, it seems clear that the mounting governmental debt and the increasing cost of welfare programs (both fueled by inflation) could have a substantial influence on education in the near future. Since many program and curriculum improvements require additional funds, teachers and parents should be mindful that they will need to have proposals for curriculum improvement that are both appealing and carefully designed so that they can compete successfully for the limited monies available.

---

[18]The hidden or latent curriculum, as discussed here, is a term that refers to what children and youth learn because of the attitudes and values for which the school stands.

[19]Mihajlo Mesarovic and Eduard Pestel, *Mankind at the Turning Point: The Second Report to the Club of Rome.* New York: E. P. Dutton & Co./Reader's Digest Press, 1974. 210 pp.

[20]See Geoffrey Barraclough, "Wealth and Power, The Politics of Food and Oil," *New York Review of Books* 22:23–30; August 7, 1976.

The potentially serious problems of funding require additional comment. In the first decade of expanded welfare provisions—from 1964 to 1974—program costs increased from $13.3 to $111.5 billion, a jump of 738 percent. In the fiscal year ending on June 30, 1976, $116 billion in the federal budget was absorbed by subsidies for veterans, the postal service, medicare, and so on.[21] Education costs, public and private, during the same interval, July 1, 1975 to June 30, 1976, amounted to another $108 billion for local, state, and federal support for programs extending from elementary through postsecondary education.[22] These figures, and their long-range projections, plus the increasing funds that social security will require, underscore the need for tough-minded curriculum and program developments that can attract support.

So much for a brief résumé of a few selected forces or developments with a probable bearing on the fabric of life in the United States between the late 1970's and the late 1990's. Let us now turn to the 28 cardinal premises generated by the NEA's panelists.

CRITERIA FOR EVALUATING EDUCATIONAL PROGRAMS THAT ARE REAFFIRMED BY THE 28 CARDINAL PREMISES. The educational premises presented in Chapter V covered a broad spectrum. It seems appropriate, therefore, to sort them out and determine what criteria they provide for parents and teachers seeking to judge the merits of proposed curriculum changes in their schools.

A re-reading of the premises suggests at least ten characteristics or criteria for judging a good program of instruction.[23] With these criteria in mind, participants in program planning can begin to reach conclusions on two questions: (a) To what extent do our present programs and our plans for the future meet the ten criteria? and, (b) What can be changed in the content and organization of

---

[21]The data cited were compiled by *U.S. News and World Report* from published federal reports.

[22]The cost estimate was made by Dr. Terrel Bell, one of the NEA Pre-Planning Committee members and then U.S. Commissioner of Education.

[23]A number of the ten criteria which follow, in one form or another, have been advocated or discussed by teachers and parents for some years. The lack of novelty in these instances serves to emphasize their enduring importance.

our curriculum further to improve the educational experiences of learners of all ages?

The criteria that suggest themselves, and the 28 cardinal premises from which they were inferred, are as follows:

1. The educational program consistently fosters a climate in which human relationships are strengthened and extended. The development of good relations in family, school, and community are a prerequisite and a foundation for a positive, harmonious spirit of global community (premises I and II).

2. The curriculum is designed methodically to develop an *awareness* of the meaning of democracy, an insightful *loyalty* to its principles, and *skill* in the exercise of its principles (premises I, II, V, XX, XXI, XXIV, XXV, XXVI, XXVII, and XXVIII).

3. The effective school environment contributes significantly and deliberately to mental, emotional, and physical health (premises VI, VIII, IX, and XIV).

4. The organization of the curriculum and of the school insures the greatest possible degree of equity in the opportunities provided among the unequal[24] children and youth whom it inevitably enrolls (premises III, IV, X, XI, XII, and XIX).

5. Methods of instruction and the schools' intellectual climate emphasize inquiry and discovery approaches to learning whenever this is feasible (premises XV, XX, XXI and XXV).

6. In addition to process and inquiry skills, the instruction develops a command of requisite skills and a fund of knowledge that have relevance and meaning for learners of any age and that also serve to make the individual of use to both self and society (premises XIII, XVIII, XXVI, and XXVII).

7. The curriculum provides guidelines for the continuing development of social, scientific, and economic literacy for persons of all ages. This includes realistic and critically important insights needed for a beginning understanding of such biospheric problems as pollution, resource depletion, the spread of sophisticated weapons, population trends, and hunger (premises V, XVI, XXII, and XXIV).

8. The administrative organization of the school and its curriculum policies help to create warm, strong school and family relationships that serve reasonable parental aspirations and also increase the odds that the learner will be able to live a satisfy-

---

[24]The term "unequal" is used to emphasize that socioeconomic status, physical disabilities or skills, family resources or problems, and other handicaps or advantages create needs and lacks among all learners.

ing, contributive life both in school and in the future (premises XVII and XIX).

9. School policies encourage continuous, in-depth, and personalized assessment of human development including, but not totally limited to, academic progress and with due recognition for the point that *all* normal children deviate from "average" behavior and performance (premises VI, VIII, IX, XIX, and the premises stressed by youth).

10. The policies and program of the school help to educate teachers on an in-service basis as they participate in the activities which the administrative and curricular structure encourages (implicit in all premises).

A TIMETABLE FOR EDUCATIONAL CHANGE.   Traditionally, change has been slow in the United States. Most persons born in the 1850's died in a world quite similar to the one in which they had first seen the light of day. Developments in education were leisurely, too. This is illustrated by the seven editions of the McGuffey Readers. They were first published in 1836, and about 122 million copies were used during the next 84 years. Although many new editions appeared, generations of American boys and girls were exposed to the same materials. One must conclude that one reason for the long acceptance of McGuffey's selections was that life-styles and value patterns in the United States didn't change much in basic ways for many decades.

While Americans' lives began to change more rapidly in the 20th century, it was in the years after 1940 that the Big Change began. In the lifetime of a person who had a 36th birthday in 1976, the following had occurred:

- Telecommunication became, for practical purposes, instantaneous.
- The speed of information data processing increased one million-fold.
- The rate of population increase went up a thousandfold.
- The power of weapons increased from the World War II blockbuster to multimegaton H-bombs of almost incalculable power.
- Jet aircraft, radar, and color TV became commonplace.
- Major organs such as the human heart were transplanted.
- Moon and Martian landings were successfully completed.

The list could go on and on, but the point has been made. In one brief lifetime more technological, social, political, economic, and biological innovations and changes doubtless have occurred than in the previous 5000 years! This suggests that educational lag must be reduced lest we end up by planning for the 1980's and 1990's the schools that were needed in the 1950's.

The fact of rapid change brings to mind the need for parents and teachers, as they explore program developments suggested by the 28 cardinal premises, to establish a realistic timetable for innovation in their local districts. While planning in a society characterized by and plagued by uncertainty cannot be governed by a frozen, inflexible schedule, target dates for changes are nonetheless essential.

They are essential because so much remains to be accomplished by 2001 that delays could seriously impair U.S. opportunities in the next century. The NEA panelists' images of the next 25 years, as summarized in Chapter II, suggest that major social decisions must be made with respect to improving our present naive uses of technology, for meeting the human needs of the old, the very young, and the disadvantaged, for developing international relationships that reflect the growing mutual need for one another in the human community, for controlling insupportable population growth, and many similar challenges.[25] We have perhaps a dozen years in which to reach policy decisions and another dozen years in which to implement the decisions that are needed to insure that the 21st century is a decent and humane one for men and women everywhere. All educational agencies, and especially the schools with their highly prepared personnel, almost inevitably will be needed and involved not only in the processes of education but in influencing policy development such as the times require.

Under such circumstances, a three-phase timetable for change and intervention suggests itself: (1) a preintervention period extending for five years (1977–1982); (2) an interval for exploring options, lasting about ten years (1982–1992), and (3) a critical period of indefinite duration during which reforms such as those suggested by the 28 cardinal premises are continually evaluated and consistently refined.

---

[25]For a more complete list of the social decisions confronting U.S. citizens, see Chapter XII in William Van Til, ed., *Issues in Secondary Education,* 75th Yearbook of the NSSE. Chicago: University of Chicago Press, 1976.

During phase 1, the present status of promising proposals for reforms in education would be assessed, new ideas generated, and vintage ideas re-examined to ascertain whether desirable ones had been overlooked or neglected. It would be a time of tooling up for fundamental reorganization of content, structure, administrative policy, and teacher education.

Phase 2, the interval of options, would involve wide-scale introduction of seminal ideas. Because of the commitment to *process*—to the planning in which parents and teachers should engage and to which they would bring their personal kowledge of unique local problems, needs, and opportunities—it would be inconsistent to attempt to suggest what these innovations might be. One generalization does seem in order, however. During the interval of options, parents and teachers should not think of "schools for tomorrow" merely as today's schools with their problems removed. As a part of the total educational resources of the nation, as agencies providing a lifelong, seamless educational continuum for learners of all ages, schools will have to differ markedly from the institutions they are today.

Probing the future is a bit like looking up the trunk of a leafy tree in midsummer. We can see just so far, and then the branches fork, and our vision is obscured by the thickening foliage. Applying this analogy to phase 3, the period of educational (and social) uncertainties with which we will live after the new millennium begins, one can say little about the alternatives that might emerge. And, as previously noted, it would be a presumptuous exercise in futility for us, after advocating processes of local developmental planning, to attempt to provide answers!

Chapter VIII does *not* propose to offer gratuitous advice on curriculum change. It does, however, explore what the 28 premises suggest—in the most general terms—about the kinds of experiences and content that should prove to be of value to learners of all ages.

CHAPTER VIII
CURRICULUM CONTENT
THAT ANTICIPATES TOMORROW

As they work together at the many tasks of curriculum development for a society in transition, it is important for parents to share an understanding of many of the practices and concepts related to the term *curriculum.* An old oriental proverb tells us that the beginning of wisdom is calling things by their right names. This is good advice, so let us begin Chapter VIII with a sharp look at the meaning of *curriculum.*

UNDERSTANDING THE MEANING OF CUR-RICULUM. An umpire was once asked to explain how he defined *ball* and *strike* when the sphere twirled past the batter. "They don't mean anything," he said, "until I calls 'em!"

In some ways, finding a definition for *curriculum* is similar to the umpire's definition. The term often means what parents or teachers intend it to mean! To many people it simply refers to the content of instruction—the subject matter. As two authors phrased it in rather elaborate rhetoric, the curriculum thus becomes "a planned series of encounters between a neophyte [the student] and the communities of symbolic discourse [the content]."[1]

Again, there are writers, parents, and teachers who have a broader interpretation and think of the curriculum as "those experiences of the child which the school in any way utilizes or attempts to influence."[2] Other definitions range from "the design of a social group for the educational experiences of their children in

---

[1]Arthur R. King, Jr., and John A. Brownell, *The Curriculum and the Disciplines of Knowledge.* New York: John Wiley and Sons, 1966. p. 213.

[2]Dorris Lee and Murray Lee, *The Child and His Curriculum.* New York: D. Appleton Co., 1940. p. 165.

school"[3] to the idea that the curriculum consists of the learner's in-school experiences that have modified her/his behavior—a definition suggesting that there is an under-the-skin curriculum for each child.[4]

For practical purposes, in the pages that follow, *curriculum* will mean *a written guide or outline which parents and teachers have developed cooperatively. It is, in other words, a means used to specify the aims, materials, and procedures of instruction which promise to help teachers develop good learning experiences for children.*

THE SEVEN CARDINAL PRINCIPLES AS CURRICULUM GUIDELINES. The NEA panelists almost universally affirmed that the seven cardinal principles (or goals) had retained their taxonomic value and still were useful as labels. The panelists' tapes also suggest, as indicated in Chapter IV, that the principles have acquired a number of new and broadened meanings. If parents and teachers at the grassroots level generally agree that these seven goals provide valid curriculum guidelines, the question then becomes one of *determining* content—of deciding on the materials and procedures of instruction. It is at this juncture that the 28 cardinal premises begin to prove their practical merit. Local curriculum planners should find it helpful (or, at the very least, stimulating!) to ask, What do the 28 premises suggest for the learning experiences of children, youth, and adult learners in our community?

FROM PREMISES TO PRACTICES: PROBLEMS IN PRESCRIPTION. As parents and teachers examine and evaluate local curriculum guides and as they seek to revise them or to develop new ones, it probably will become apparent that recasting the 28 cardinal premises into recommended practices is by no means simple. At least three questions are likely to develop:

1.   Are the 28 premises, or at least a substantial number of them, acceptable in our community?

---

[3] George A. Beauchamp, *Planning the Elementary Curriculum.* Boston: Allyn & Bacon, 1965. p. 41.

[4] L. Thomas Hopkins, *Interaction: The Democratic Process.* Boston: D. C. Heath & Co., 1941. p. 443.

2. What general course of action do the premises suggest when curriculum changes are contemplated: (a) to schools, and (b) to other educational agencies?

3. Since communities—like humans—are unique, what changes in policies and practices seem likely to improve local educational agencies, including the schools?

These three queries point up the problems of curriculum prescriptions and the uniquely personal nature of local curriculum initiation and development. For instance, consider premise XV: *When and where teaching and learning occur must not be bounded either by the school's walls or by our preconceived ideas as to what should be learned at the once-traditional age for learning it.* If a group of curriculum planners—teachers, parents, youth—decide to devise and to explore expanded teaching-learning experiences in the "school without walls" of the real world, what is planned will vary greatly, say, between a rural school district in southern Indiana, an independent school in Manhattan, a large secondary school in Chicago, or a magnet school in a predominantly Latino neighborhood in Houston.

THE NEED TO PERSONALIZE LEARNING.   Not only do school districts provide a highly varied educational terrain—children and youth, too, provide a world of diversity even within a classroom populated by students from roughly the same socioeconomic stratum. As suggested in the 28 cardinal premises, there is therefore a great need to *personalize* rather than to *individualize* instruction. This is a highly important point for local curriculum planners to keep in mind. The distinctions between the terms *personalized* and *individualized*—as seen by a number of the NEA panelists—also need to be clearly understood.

Historically, attempts to individualize teaching and learning began to capture attention early in the century when Frederic Burk, president of the San Francisco State Normal School, prepared an influential pamphlet with a title that could well have been selected in the 1970's: *Lockstep Schooling and a Remedy.* One of the persons on whom his ideas had a powerful impact was Carleton W. Washburne who, in 1919, had an opportunity (in the Winnetka, Illinois, public schools) to develop what he called self-instructional materials.

As Washburne recalls it in his autobiography, Winnetka's early crude materials "made it possible for a teacher with thirty to forty children in a classroom to allow each child to work at his own pace on assignments which, as nearly as we could estimate, were fitted to his individual capacity."[5]

Classical individualization, however, as in Winnetka, was designed to help *all* children acquire a *similar* cultural heritage and a comparable body of basic skills—but at different rates of speed dictated by presumed differences in ability. Personalized learning, while clearly recognizing the fact of individual differences, envisions a curriculum in which children and youth are not herded along the same academic routes and where the effort is not made to get them to the "proper" grade level on norm-referenced tests. The 28 premises *do not* downgrade excellence. They *do* imply again and again that young people should not be expected to be in the same educational slots and performing in the same fashion at approximately the same age—a concept that is both impossible and absurd.

But polemics directed against herding children and youth—as if they were cattle—into classes that remind one of academic feedlots leave unanswered the all-important question of how to cope with the problems of creating genuinely personalized programs. *Patently, prescriptions cannot be compounded and dispensed in a report like this one because to do so would both (a) disregard the importance of process—of working together in local groups, and (b) deny the unique nature and needs of each child and the differences among schools.*

What can be offered, and what is attempted in the remaining pages of Chapter VIII, is, first, to examine some of the general attitudinal outcomes (in *addition* to skills and knowledge) that the good curriculum, circa 1976–2001, might seek to provide through locally determined content and experiences. Second, we will examine briefly a few ways in which traditional curricular and organizational structures in U.S. schools might be modified so as to serve parental aspirations, teachers' ability to work more effectively, and the well-being of learners at all levels.

In both instances, ideas in the 28 cardinal premises and values in

---

[5]Carleton W. Washburne, "An Autobiographical Sketch," in Robert J. Havighurst and Herman C. Richey, eds., *Leaders in American Education,* Seventieth Yearbook, Part II. Chicago: The University of Chicago Press, 1971. p. 467.

the recast seven cardinal principles serve as the base for the proposals that follow.

SOME CONJECTURES REGARDING CURRICULUM OUTCOMES RELATED TO LEARNERS' ATTITUDES.

During the present period, many developments are occurring almost at once in the United States and in many parts of the world. These changes require that all learners acquire an ability to participate, to reach decisions, and to carry out these decisions. Let us review a few of them quickly:

- Economic institutions are being restructured.
- After decades of competition for world markets, governments and corporations are reviewing and manipulating export policies governing such resources as oil, natural gas, or phosphates.
- Urban deterioration continues.
- Environmentalists warn that new less-growth or nongrowth lifestyles may be essential and that voluntary frugality in our consumption patterns is in order.
- There is a regional oversupply of degree-holding *academically* skilled labor, but a need for able, *technically* skilled nondegree workers.
- Concepts of work and leisure are being re-examined.
- Major power-and-control shifts are taking place from the local to the transnational level.
- The problems of the poor in the United States show signs of becoming less closely associated with race and more closely associated with socioeconomic class status.

All developments such as these, as they have in the past, will continue to be powerfully influenced by the future attitudes and values of today's learners. And the schools have not done a spectacular job—nor have related educational agencies—in providing the experiences on which socially and economically sound attitudes depend. As Alvin Toffler phrased it:

> Millions pass through the educational system without once having been forced to search out the contradictions in their own value systems, to probe their own life goals deeply, or even to discuss these matters candidly with adults and peers.[6]

---

[6] Alvin Toffler, *Future Shock*. New York: Random House, 1970. p. 417.

In curriculum planning, in whatever ways we can devise, parents and teachers need to begin to reach conclusions as to what experiences with *content,* with *human relations skills,* and with *ideas* can help alleviate and then defuse the American and world-wide value crises which have been heightened in the past decade.[7] This means seeking factual data and honestly confronting learners, once they have acquired sufficient maturity, about what to do about the controversial status of U.S. consumption. As Ward and Dubos[8] have pointed out, if a U.S. baby and a baby born in a mud-hut village of India had their consumption compared over a 68-year lifetme, the American would consume 500 kilos of resources such as coal, iron, aluminum, and so on, to every one kilo consumed by the Indian. Indeed, U.S. citizens are high consumers even when compared with other developed, capitalist economies. In 1974–75, per capita consumption of energy in the United States was three times as great as that of the Swiss, for instance, and double that of the West Germans.

What, then, are some of the kinds of attitudinal changes in our young that might be contemplated through changes in our *own* thinking and through our educational agencies? Quite possibly, local discussion will lead to the conclusion that, by both the precept and the example of adults and educational agencies, positive attitudes to be developed through the experiences which the curriculum provides for an imperiled planet will include:

1. An appreciation for the merits of an improved service society—one in which even more social productivity is obtained through changes and refinements in social work, improved medical care, child care, opportunities for mature and senior learners, and so on[9]

---

[7] For an elaboration of the contemporary value crises, their origin, and possible choices in coping with them, see the writer's report to the U.S. Commissioner of Education, published by Phi Delta Kappa (Harold G. Shane, *The Educational Significance of the Future.* Bloomington, Indiana: Phi Delta Kappa, 1973. 116 pp.).

[8] See Barbara Ward and René Dubos, *Only One Earth: The Care and Maintenance of a Small Planet.* New York: W. W. Norton & Co., 1972. 225 pp.

[9] The United States has enormous untapped human resources for a more service-minded society in the coming decades. The prospects for a four-day week, an increase of nearly 50 percent in the post-65 age group, and more service from teenagers "on break" from their formal schooling promise to provide low-cost or no-cost people power as our attitudes toward what is of worth begin to change.

2.   Ways of improving further the contributions which American mass media are capable of making to the general education and information of millions. What we show we appreciate by the way we teleview will determine our TV fare

3.   Awareness of our need to regain our loss of amenities and gracious living due to crowding, mass production, and low-quality entertainment, and to restore to family life the warmth which being together can bring

4.   Recognition for the need, however painful, to "true-cost" our products: the idea that to the price of the things we consume—say, capital goods such as automobiles or air conditioners—we must add the cost of restoring to the biosphere (insofar as we can) those materials extracted from it. This involves the need to recycle, to avoid conspicuous waste, to reclaim and to reforest, and to end our "throw-away society," as Toffler labeled it

5.   An appreciation for excellence and quality reflected in support for the development or rediscovery of products that are engineered and manufactured to reverse the planned obsolescence in much of what we own

6.   A willingness to come to grips in the next several decades with our present economic dependence on the perpetual unrestricted growth doctrine which assumes that our personal and financial well-being, including full employment, depends on greater and greater consumption rather than on selective growth that husbands and restores resources

7.   An appreciation for the behavioral and value differences in the ethnic-cultural fabric of one's fellow citizens and among other humans in the world community—plus respect for these poly-cultural textures.

Other possible attitudinal changes in ourselves and our youth could be inferred from the 28 cardinal premises in great numbers. However, the point already should be made that in curriculum planning it is what parents and teachers value (as shown by what they *do,* not what they *say*) that has the greatest effect on the way youth's attitudes take shape. As the writer has noted elsewhere in an abridgement of this NEA Project report:

The task of helping youth form new values is more easily described than implemented. It requires wholesome adult example rather than phony preachments. It is a test of *adult* wisdom, maturity, moral courage, and "biospheric morality" even more than it is a test of the young.[10]

SOME SPECULATION WITH REGARD TO THE STRUCTURE AND ORGANIZATION OF THE CURRICULUM IN THE 1980'S.

Scholars have identified and reached something approaching a consensus on the areas or realms of knowledge. B. Othanel Smith, a member of the NEA Project Pre-Planning Committee, has enumerated them and commented on them clearly and succinctly:[11]

> First are the *arts,* including architecture, choreography, graphic arts, landscaping, music, literature, and so on. Second are the *basics,* which include the physical, biological, psychological, and social sciences. Third, the sciences that deal with the *past.* Among these are geology, cosmology, evolution, and the accounts of man's cultural evolution. Fourth are the *welfare* sciences. Among these are medicine, technology, agriculture, peace, and national defense. Fifth are the *regulative* sciences. Among these are jurisprudence, political science, economics, management, and administration. Sixth are the *dissemination* sciences. Among these are education, journalism, library sciences, and mass communication. Seventh are the *symbolic* sciences. These include mathematics, languages, linguistics, logic, and so on. Eighth are the *methodological* sciences—taxonomy, and general methodology—which have to do with promotion of the growth of all arts and sciences. And finally there are the *integrative* sciences, which include philosophy, theology, and general systems. I do not see how the schools can meet the needs of the future with a curriculum that emphasizes the symbolic and basic sciences and the sciences of the past and neglects the welfare sciences, the regulative sciences, the disseminative sciences, the arts, the sciences of methodology, and, most important of all, the integrative sciences.

Probably few parents or teachers would disagree with Professor Smith's conclusion as to the need for U.S. education to encompass

---

[10]Harold G. Shane, "America's Next 25 Years: Some Implications for Education," *Phi Delta Kappan* 58:81; September 1976.

[11]B. Othanel Smith in a letter to the writer dated May 17, 1976. Dr. Smith's suggestions were stimulated by Joseph T. Tykociner, author of *Outline of Zetetics* and originator of the taxonomy.

all nine realms, providing that due allowance is made for variations in the maturity and the motivation of learners. The classification also is highly valuable when the scope of the curriculum is evaluated in the local community.

How effectively the nine areas make their respective contributions to the individual and to the educational mainstream, however, is influenced by the *structure* of the curriculum and the administrative *organization* into which they are phased. Attention now comes to a focus on some changes which some of the 28 premises suggest for the development of *the seamless lifelong educational continuum* on a year-round basis. (See premises III and IV.)

In most of our schools, a graded system presently is followed; this can be represented as in Figure 1. If, however, one begins to think in terms of opportunities for learning throughout life— including opportunities for the very young and for the mature (30 plus) or senior (60 plus) learners, our model changes, as in Figure 2.

An education that really helps to prevent future problems during lifelong learning must allow for the child to be born as defect-free as possible. That is why the model of the educational continuum begins shortly after conception with the "−8" months! This is meant to suggest that parent education and careful physical examinations, with remedial follow-up as needed, are an essential part of being born as close to free and equal as possible in the United States. In effect in the model, provision for the future ability of the young person to profit from his or her education is made even before birth through adequate prenatal care.

A careful examination of Figure 2 also indicates that when a child reaches approximately age two, a *nonschool preschool* experience

FIGURE 1

Current Grade Levels

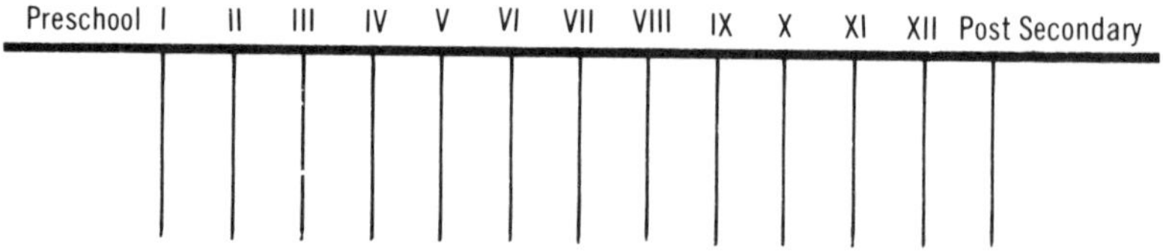

Preschool	I	II	III	IV	V	VI	VII	VIII	IX	X	XI	XII	Post Secondary

FIGURE 2

Current Grade Levels

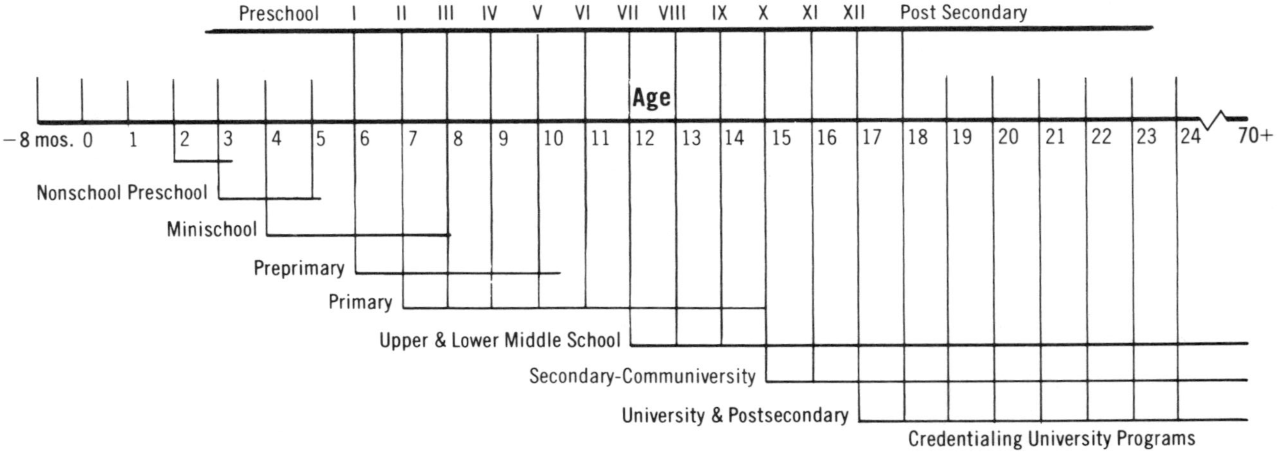

CARL A. RUDISILL LIBRARY
LENOIR RHYNE COLLEGE

begins. This term refers to a social investment in as many mutual and physical checks as are feasible: vocabulary development, dentition, blood chemistry, reflexes, and the like, plus follow-up therapy or remedial care as needed. Such an examination also should serve to help identify any signs of the persistent problems of child-battering and parental neglect.

The term *minischool*[12] for the three-year-olds in Figure 2 refers to the beginning of learning experiences under direct school auspices for those children who are ready to profit from it.[13] The minischool program, or segment in a continuum, provides a good nursery-level education that emphasizes the rich, developmental input which provides the quality that the schools later measure and label *intelligence.*

The preprimary years provided for four and fives in the model are distinctly different in spirit from the kindergartens of the 1970's which presently serve these age levels. They represent an interval of time which would vary (just as the duration of nursery school should vary) with a given child's readiness to cope successfully with beginning reading, numbers, and other tasks associated with six-year-oldness. Most boys and girls, perhaps four out of five or nine out of ten, would spend two years in the preprimary unit. But the child who matures rapidly physically, socially, and intellectually, might spend as little as 12 to 18 months in this ungraded group, then be *transposed*[14] to the primary school to mix with sixes and sevens because her/his behavior is more mature than that of most five-year-olds.

Conversely, a slow-maturing, disadvantaged, or handicapped child might spend three rather than two years in the preprimary program for four- and five-year-olds. When professional teacher-judgment has determined the timing, at age six, seven, or even

---

[12] I am indebted to Professor Bernard Spodek of the University of Illinois, Urbana, for much of the early childhood terminology used here.

[13] Since children mature at different rates, patently a set age for beginning nursery school should vary, too.

[14] *Transpose* means to change order or position. In a lifelong learning continuum, based on continuous progress, presumably the artificial annual promotions now widely used would be replaced by a policy of moving (transposing) children to new groups or levels at any time when professional teacher-judgment suggests such a shift is appropriate.

eight, such children would be transposed to work with children at whose performance levels they are likely to operate successfully.

The model of the early childhood education years, extending approximately through age eight, is portrayed more explicitly in the three-dimensional model shown in Figure 3.[15]

This supplementary model not only is designed to show that the child *might* spend from one to three or even four to five years in the preprimary continuum. It also is intended to convey the idea that the principle of personalized progress, or *flow,* in the learning continuum would govern the number of years spent by a given boy or girl in the primary school or, later, in the secondary school.

In fine, some learners in today's schools, hemmed in by promotion policies and inflexible requirements, spend *more time* marking time than they need to. Others have *too little time* to develop the competencies, the confidence, and the general maturity needed for a subsequently satisfying and contributive life. The stigma of failure or the erosive fear that one lacks ability and worth are prices often paid by the slow-maturing and the disadvantaged under these circumstances.

The NEA panelists' concept of lifelong learning (premise III), for practical purposes suggests schooling in which the *age range* in a given group of learners (beginning with the preprimary four- and five-year-olds) *will increase* as the years pass. At the same time, *dif-*

FIGURE 3

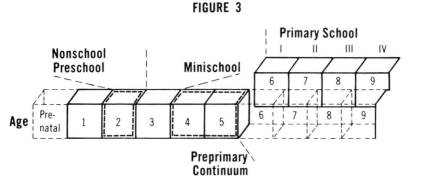

---

[15] Adapted from the writer's report to the U.S. Commissioner of Education, *The Educational Significance of the Future, op. cit.*

ferences in the social and academic skills in this group of learners will decrease.[16] Figure 4 shows the way in which age overlap might increase in the elementary and secondary school years.

At present in the United States, most first graders are six years old, fourth graders ten years old, and so on. In the continuum depicted, the nongraded primary segment would enroll rapid-maturing young people as young as five as well as slow developers

FIGURE 4

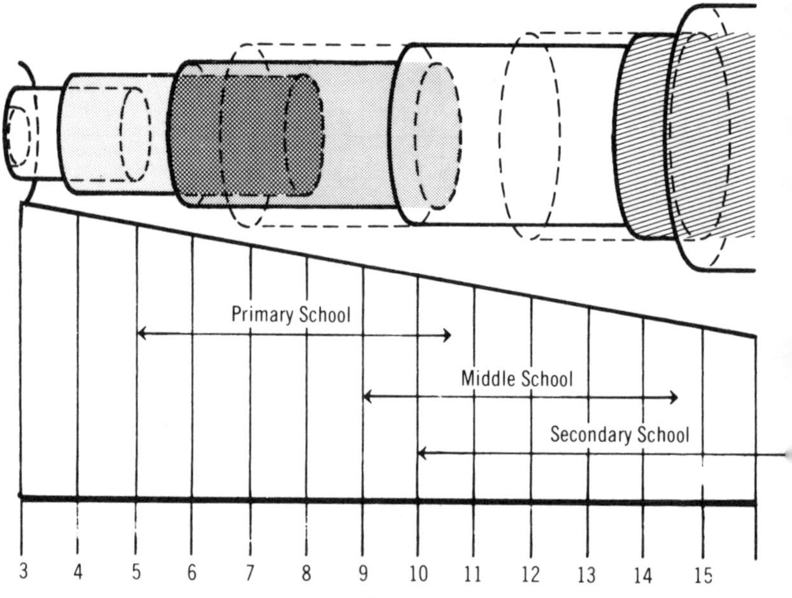

Primary School

Middle School

Secondary School

3 4 5 6 7 8 9 10 11 12 13 14 15

Age

---

[16]It should clearly be understood that speculation about increased age and decreased ranges in performance differs completely from traditional ability grouping in self-contained or departmentalized classes and based on norm-referenced test scores or IQ scores. Cross-age groupings would be associated with short-term activities and projects, as in so-called "open schools." In skill subjects, learners of comparable ability would work together in ephemeral groups of a few hours to several months' duration.

up to, say, age eleven. The middle school, basically four years in length, would encompass an age span of eight- to fourteen-year-olds whose performance was that of ten- to thirteen-year-olds. Enrollments in the secondary years of the continuum could, in this interpretation of lifelong learning, extend from rapid-maturing elevens through the ranks of mature (30 plus) learners to the senior (60 plus) learners continuing their education on a personal-choice basis.

The structure contemplated in the conjectures presented could extend through the postsecondary years with the same flow and flexibility. It also contemplates keeping the school open on a year-round basis, although a given student or teacher would be present for approximately 185 days.

If the several models above are combined, one ends up with the model of the seamless lifelong educational continuum shown in Figure 5.[17] The reader will note that university and other forms of postsecondary education have been added to the model. Provision is also made for credentialing programs from which teachers, physicians, architects, engineers, nurses, lawyers, dentists, and other professionals are graduated.

A fine line exists between prescription and speculations designed to trigger discussion of curriculum content and structure. The intent in this section is not to prescribe but to stimulate imagination and to provoke discussion in local school districts of curriculum change and of the inevitable structural changes that accompany it. An effort also has been made to re-emphasize the point that tomorrow's schools probably will be quite different from today's—and that they surely will not merely be today's schools with a few of their more troublesome problems smoothed over or removed.

SOME IMPLICATIONS FOR TEACHING AND LEARN-ING NOT BOUNDED BY THE SCHOOL'S WALLS. Many of the tapes made by NEA panelists were conspicuously clear on one point preserved in premise XV.[18] This premise, like the premise pertaining to the lifelong educational continuum, has important im-

---

[17] Figure 5, and the parts of it reproduced as Figures 1, 2, and 4, as well as Figure 6, is designed by the author and was originally drawn by Steve Soulier.

[18] For an elaboration of premise XIV, see Chapter VIII.

FIGURE 5

The Seamless Lifelong Educational Curriculum

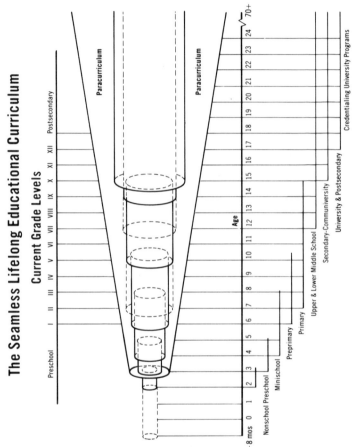

plications for the curriculum planning in which parents and teachers are likely to become involved. The concluding section of this chapter of curricular conjectures directs attention toward the ways in which schools might seek further to utilize educational resources and the agencies to which, as one panelist phrased it, the schools are losing the monopoly which they enjoyed in the 1950's.

In approaching this topic, it will be helpful to think of the *para-curriculum,* a term used to describe the body of out-of-school experiences that help to strengthen the intellectual ability, general background, and coping powers of learners of all ages.[19] It embodies the idea that schooling provides only a part of the experience that adds up to the learner's total education, and, unlike elementary, secondary, and postsecondary education, input from paracurricular sources extends virtually from birth to death.

For a number of years—long before the word paracurriculum was coined—schools at all levels, of course, have made deliberate use of nonschool resources. Museums, resource persons invited to share special knowledge or skills with students, libraries, the zoo, public concerts, and the world of work as represented by firehouse or supermarket or airport are representative of such resource use. At the postsecondary level, medical and nursing programs use the resources of clinic and hospitals, and apprenticeship or on-the-job preparation of teachers and engineers is widely accepted.

Figure 6 again portrays the lifelong educational continuum but this time with arrows added to suggest how the paracurriculum— the out-of-school learning resources—can be linked to the process of schooling. Note that these resources are portrayed in such a way as to indicate that they are used even with three- to five-year-olds. The fact that arrows point in two directions show that beyond-school-walls learning penetrates the paracurriculum, as when a middle school group visits the museum, and that paracurricular or "real world" resources also permeate in-school learning, as when a fireman or police officer comes to visit a primary school group.

The model also is intended to suggest that schools and other educational agencies can and should arrange infinite exit and re-entry privileges throughout learner's lifetimes. The school here is

---

[19]Increasingly used since the early 1970's, *paracurriculum* is derived from the Greek prefix *para,* which means *beside of* or *alongside of,* plus *curriculum. Parapro-fessional* is a familiar, analogous term.

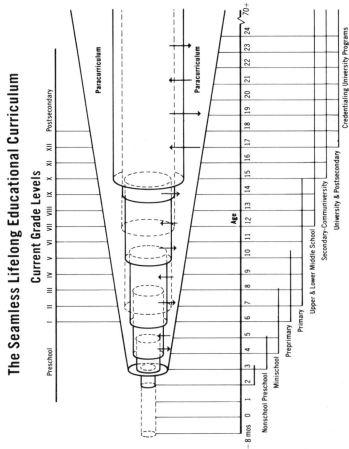

FIGURE 6

The Seamless Lifelong Educational Curriculum

also conceived as having the role of a participatory planner and as a broker in arranging for learners to spend time in the world of work as an integral part of their personalized educations.[20] As Figure 6 illustrates, world-of-work experiences (either with or without pay) might either permanently or temporarily replace or parallel in-school learning for teenage youth. This lateral move into vocationally useful activity, when "brokered" by the school, would presumably involve family understanding and consent, careful professional judgment and counseling, and close working relationships with assorted employers and such social agencies as hospitals, libraries, and welfare offices which have a genuine need for and opportunities for youth to serve in useful roles.[21]

An integral part of the out-of-school learning experience, it must be noted, is the *planned* exit and re-entry feature and safeguards against any exploitation of youth such as existed prior to child-labor reforms instituted early in the present century. In their teens and after more than a decade of personalized progress in the continuum, adolescents or older youth would, through the good offices of the school, move from cirricular to paracurricular learning *and vice versa.* The dropout phenomena would undoubtedly be alleviated in the process, and the re-entry experience made inconspicuous as persons of widely varied ages develop the habit of life-long learning in or through an array of educational agencies, among which schools would not only remain highly visible but would also become increasingly important.

SUMMARY. This chapter on curriculum content for tomorrow, after recognizing the several meanings of *curriculum,* indicated how the 28 cardinal premises could serve as guidelines as parents and teachers contemplated changes and innovations. At the same time care was taken to avoid prescribing specific content out of

---

[20]The out-of-school paracurricular experience for high school students at the junior-senior level or for college freshmen or sophomores has been discussed and advocated by Professor James Coleman, author of the Coleman Report. (See "The Problems of Youth," *Today's Education* 64:74–80; March–April 1975.)

[21]Chapter IX identifies and expands on ways in which the school might provide important learnings and opportunities for socially useful service in related educational agencies.

deference to the community's privilege to reach decisions that best serve local needs.

Heed was given, however, (a) to the need for the learner's curriculum to be *personalized* and (b) to the importance of developing thoughtful, socially desirable attitudes through whatever content ultimately is incorporated in the nine areas of knowledge introduced in Chapter VIII. The closing section attempted through the use of illustrative models to clarify and to expand on the NEA panelists' premises that education should be encouraged on a life-long basis and that learning resources beyond the classroom walls should be utilized even more than at present to reinforce, extend, and motivate in-school learning.

CHAPTER IX
THE SCHOOL AS A PERSONALIZED
LEARNING CENTER

Many years ago, in 1897, when philosopher John Dewey wrote *My Pedagogic Creed*[1], he spoke of the school as being "that form of community life in which all those agencies are concentrated that will be most effective in bringing the child to share in the inherited resources of the [human] race. . . ."

Some years later, in *Democracy and Education,* Dewey went on to identify four duties for our schools: (a) to provide a simplified environment, (b) to serve as a medium for introducing the young to aspects of the culture which are decent, just, beautiful, and honorable, (c) to help children understand the polycultural and multiethnic elements in the environment, and (d) to coordinate within the individual the diverse social environments he is entering so that he will understand and be sensitive to them.[2] These points were made over 60 years ago at about the same time the original seven cardinal principles were being developed by the NEA commission.

Continuing to use the cardinal *principles* and the 28 cardinal *premises* as guidelines, it seems helpful, in the concluding chapter of this NEA project report, to consider the ways in which the school can be used in the 1970's and 1980's as an effective teaching aid in attaining the four duties suggested by Dewey. His four points, like the seven principles, seem to have retained their validity despite the passage of time!

For purposes of discussion by teachers and parents, some of the ways in which it may be possible for schools to develop into

---

[1]*My Pedagogic Creed,* with a preface by Jay Elmer Morgan (then editor of the *NEA Journal*), was published as "NEA Personal Growth Leaflet Number Nineteen," n.d.

[2]John Dewey, *Democracy and Education.* New York: Henry Holt and Co., 1916. p. 24ff.

increasingly effective centers for personalized learning are discussed under five headings:

1. The importance of community input and feedback in program development
2. The role of "basics" in the experiences of children and youth
3. Designing opportunities for widening the learner's exposure to valuable experiences
4. Developing service-learning and action-learning opportunities
5. The school as an environment for moral development.

The ideas expressed in these five headings, insofar as possible, will be combined in a model of the school itself as a personalized learning center.

COMMUNITY INPUT AND FEEDBACK.   At a time when the public has been critical of U.S. schools and sometimes laggard in financial support, it is important—as school and community work together—to keep in mind the values of a close working relationship, as depicted in Chapter VI. As the persons concerned with program development work and interact, community input and feedback become an important component of our model of the school as a personalized learning center. Let us label this Component I, as in Figure 7. Patently, educational change is seriously if not hopelessly impeded without this component.

THE ROLE OF BASIC CONTENT IN PROGRAM DEVELOPMENT.   The NEA panelists, without exception, not only reaffirmed the importance of competence in the three R's but also made the point that there were "new basic skills" associated

FIGURE 7

The School
as a Personalized Learning Center

Component I

COMMUNITY INPUT and FEEDBACK

FIGURE 8

The School
as a Personalized Learning Center *(cont.)*

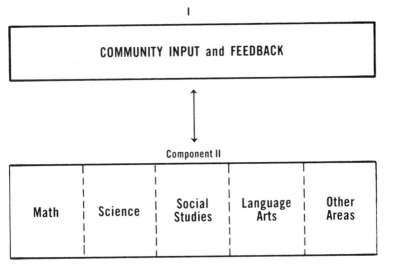

I

COMMUNITY INPUT and FEEDBACK

Component II

Math	Science	Social Studies	Language Arts	Other Areas

with the second cardinal goal, "command of fundamental processes."[3] Undoubtedly, the role of mathematics, science, the social studies, and the language arts (including stress on reading, listening, interpreting, and communicating clearly) must play a central role in any model of the school as a nourishing educational medium for human growth and development. Other areas or realms of learning—health, physical education, recreation, art, and music, for instance—also are encompassed in our expanding model. When they are added, the model assumes the form shown in Figure 8.

The two-headed arrow is intended to emphasize the importance of input and feedback *processes* and of close interaction and cooperation. The dotted as opposed to solid lines separating the content areas or realms of knowledge represent the point made by several panelists; namely, that the disciplines of knowledge are becoming

---

[3]The meaning of "command of fundamental processes" is expanded on p. 45.

more interrelated and more inclined to permeate other disciplines.[4]

INCREASING SCHOOL-RELATED OPPORTUNITIES FOR WIDENING THE LEARNER'S EXPOSURE TO VALUABLE EXPERIENCES.

Without diminishing the importance of content, the NEA panelists left little doubt that *varied* exposures to *many* experiences were important as educational offerings changed during the present era of transition.

At the primary school level, there is relatively little need for advocating and illustrating the expansion and enriching of childhood experience. For many years able, sensitive teachers have considered the many forms of program enrichment to be an integral part of teaching and learning. Objects of interest and persons of interest are introduced, and field trips may be taken to airport, zoo, or weather bureau. Whether in one-teacher classrooms or through team teaching, younger children often are with the same teacher or same group of teachers during all or most of the school day. Hence, it is fairly simple to coordinate their experiences.

During the middle school or junior high school years, and increasingly in the secondary school setting, exposures to persons and places of interest tend to be less common because they often become more difficult to coordinate. Departmental programs that compete for the students' time, the time blocks into which the day is divided, and increasing emphasis on the various areas of knowledge combine to reduce the use of the out-of-school or of paracurricular resources (as discussed in Chapter VIII).

In view of the emphasis placed on exposure to experiences that stretch the learner's knowledge, our model is now expanded to depict an "Experience-Exposure" wheel (Figure 9). The wheel, arbitrarily numbered from one to seven, is accompanied by an arrow which suggests that in a given period of time (say, four to six weeks), a short-term exposure experience aligns itself with the basic content represented by the labels *"Mathematics," "Science,"* and so on.

---

[4]The nine areas of knowledge, which extend from early beginnings in childhood through postsecondary education for senior learners, were introduced and more explicitly delineated in Chapter VIII. They are merely symbolized here with labels such as "mathematics" and "language arts."

FIGURE 9

The School
as a Personalized Learning Center *(cont.)*

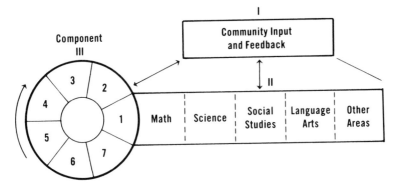

Now the reader is asked to imagine that in each numbered section of the wheel there are *experiences* rather than a number. For young adolescents between 11 and 12 or 14 and 15, these might include the following:

1. Personal typing instruction
2. Participating as junior paraprofessionals in the early childhood education programs sponsored by the school district
3. A short course on the major languages of the world, who speaks them, and how language can be used to influence behavior
4. Participating in various types of dramatic productions for presentation to classmates—in which casting might be used for placing young persons in roles that were psychologically valuable to them
5. Art-shop experiences
6. Speed reading
7. An introduction to consumer education and to propaganda analysis
8. Tutoring younger children
9. An introduction to the computer and to computer languages
10. Preparing signs and posters for appropriate school or community events or performing useful school office services
11. Providing help on the primary school playground.

As the rotating experience-exposure wheel is intended to illustrate, opportunities such as the eleven listed above would change periodically, with new opportunities clicking into place. Furthermore, their sequence and content should be both varied and personalized to provide proper matching among the learner's needs and choices, the experience-exposures, and the teacher, adult volunteer, or paraprofessional sponsoring them.

To sum up, Component III of the model should help to implement several of the 28 cardinal premises: for instance, process skills, varied routes to learning, a measure of student self-direction, personalization, more flexible grouping, an opening of diverse vocational vistas, and varied methods of instruction.

FACILITATING SERVICE LEARNING AND ACTION LEARNING UNDER SCHOOL LEADERSHIP.

For many years the importance of youth engaging in socially useful work has been discussed in the literature and occasionally has been embodied in school-sponsored projects. One of the authors of the original seven cardinal principles, William H. Kilpatrick, writing in the 1920's, saw a need to find new worthy activities for the young,[5] and Paul R. Hanna, in *Youth Serves the Community,*[6] described in detail dozens of school- and community-sponsored projects that involved the giving of worthy service by youth as society strove to cope with the problems and tragedies of the "threadbare thirties."

More recently, as noted in Chapter VIII (n. 20), James Coleman[7] in a *Today's Education* interview has advocated an out-of-school year for service and work experience for older adolescents. Alvin Toffler, discussing "The Psychology of the Future" in *Learning for Tomorrow* is even more specific. Education, he tells us:

> is not just something that happens in the head. It involves our muscles, our senses, our hormonal defenses, our total biochemistry. Nor does it occur solely *within* the individual. Education springs from the interplay between the individual and a changing environ-

[5] See his *Education for a Changing Civilization.* New York: The MacMillan Co., 1926.

[6] Paul R. Hanna, *Youth Serves the Community.* New York: D. Appleton-Century Co., 1936.

[7] James Coleman, "The Problems of Youth," *Today's Education* 64:74–80; March–April 1975.

ment. The movement to heighten future-consciousness in education, therefore, must be seen as one step toward a deep restructuring
of the links between school, colleges, universities, and the communities that surround them.[8]

If education is concerned with helping the young and old alike to
cope with the perils and problems, opportunities and responsibilities identified in Chapter II, it must shuttle back and forth
between school and the wider environment in what Toffler dubs
"action learning,"[9] involving the real world of business, politics,
pollution, and work.

Our next stage, the fourth component in the evolution of Figure
7, endeavors to portray a service and action learning wheel
analogous to the experience-exposure wheel but with different
emphases and wider purposes (Figure 10). The letters A through G
and the arrow suggesting that the service and action learnings occur
in sequence, need little explanation because of their similarity to
the operation of the experience-exposure wheel already introduced.

In general, participants in out-of-school service and action learning that is brokered or arranged by the school would be somewhat
older than the preadolescents or early adolescents involved in
experiences predominantly under the aegis or the control of the
school. They would tend to be at least 13 or 14 years of age and
usually would be older. Furthermore, the additional two-headed arrows linking the school and the community should be noted since
they emphasize the close ties with community agencies, business,
and industry that exposure experiences and service and action
learning require.

Among various kinds of service and action experiences that
could be brokered by the school during the middle–secondary–
postsecondary segments of the lifelong learning continuum, the
following suggest themselves as worthy examples:

  1. Hospital service as is presently performed by the young candy
     stripers who, in their 'teens, assume such responsibilities as
     reading to patients or helping in maternity wards

---

[8] Alvin Toffler, ed., *Learning for Tomorrow*. New York: Random House, 1974. p.
13.

[9] *Ibid.*, p. 14.

FIGURE 10

The School
As a Personalized Learning Center (cont.)

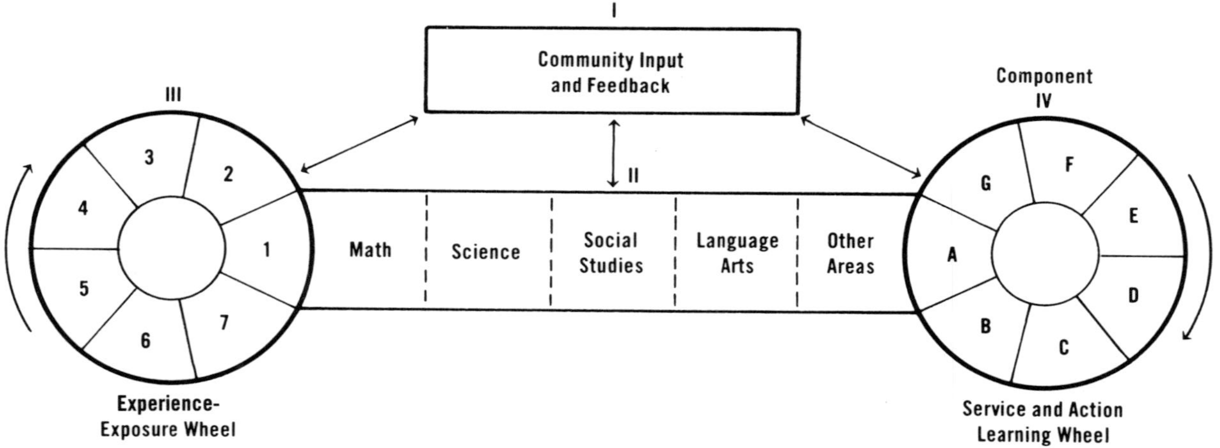

Component IV

Service and Action Learning Wheel

(Wheel segments: A, B, C, D, E, F, G)

I — Community Input and Feedback

II — Math | Science | Social Studies | Language Arts | Other Areas

III — Experience-Exposure Wheel

(Wheel segments: 1, 2, 3, 4, 5, 6, 7)

2. Library assistance in shelving books, repairing bindings, or reading during a story hour for elementary school age clients

3. Real-world employment (with careful guidance and proper safeguards) in a variety of settings ranging from professional offices through filling station, shop, or trade apprenticeships

4. Work in federal or state welfare agencies from animal shelters to food-stamp distribution and peak-season work in post offices

5. Service as paraprofessionals with teachers of younger children and including delegated work (under supervision) on the playgrounds of the school or community

6. Participation, with others of all ages, in cleanup and antipollution work

7. Affiliation with such movements as scouting and service in summer camps

8. Assisting in child-care programs, in retirement homes, or with programs for orphans

9. Involvement in church-sponsored activities, drives, and programs

10. Sharing in appropriate political activities such as get-out-the-vote drives.

An almost infinite array of alternatives for service and action learning should suggest themselves as parents, teachers, and potential sponsors (clergy, employers, agency officials, etc.) get together to plan and to implement socially useful work. There is undoubtedly a genuine need for service, either on a volunteer or on a paid basis, but of equal or greater value in the development of the young is the merit of giving of oneself. Young people in the 1970's often feel deprived of the useful roles that an earlier century provided. Service and action learning promises to provide important psychological satisfaction and maturity, which many of the young people interviewed during the NEA Project appear to seek. Furthermore, service and action learning promises to reduce the needless prolongation of adolescence and promises to reduce to a reasonable level the sorry waste of youthful energy in nonproductive activity. An added dividend: cross-age groupings of adults and adolescents serve the mutual benefit of both.

Thus far, service and action learning has been emphasized for older children and youth. This was not done with any intent to exclude primary age or even younger children from the satisfactions of serving as part of teams or task forces engaged in such activities as cleaning up litter on the school grounds. There are potential opportunities for young and old alike. The degree of responsibility, task-complexity, and locale can determine how the responsibilities of helping one another—responsibilities that reflect our humanity—best can be planned and apportioned. And in the process, U.S. schools and other educational agencies, too, have opportunities to show their institutional maturity and judgment and to move education along the lines suggested by the NEA's 28 cardinal premises.

THE SCHOOL AS AN ENVIRONMENT FOR FURTHERING MORAL DEVELOPMENT.

Since time out of mind, humans in every culture appear to have been profoundly concerned about the moral development of children and youth in the context of their particular culture. The school, in American traditions, long has been charged with the development of moral and ethical values—although the nature of the school's responsibilities has altered greatly since the 1640's when early Massachusetts Colony legislation instructed schools on how to protect the young from that "Old Deluder Satan"!

Recently the role of education, and especially of schooling, in moral education has been enhanced by the value crisis through which the nation has been passing since the early 1960's. Old verities have become as obsolete as the washboard, kerosene lamps, or a Ford Model T sedan. Yet tens of millions of U.S. citizens are in vehement disagreement as to what the good life is and how to achieve it without going bankrupt. Here, fortunately, the NEA tapes offer considerable helpful testimony.

For one thing, *moral* emerges in the panelists' dialogues as associated with *justice* and with *equity* in a world deeply troubled by hunger, population pressures, the dwindling of resources such as oil and natural gas, the immense dangers of nuclear weaponry, polluted air, and befouled oceans (which Norman Cousins, when interviewed, likened to "open sewers" because of the refuse dumped into them).

Second, either directly or indirectly, a number of panelists made the point that we can best avoid the potential problems of more and more "regulated freedom" by developing a moral *inner* discipline that makes coercive, police-statelike pressures on the group and on the individual needless.

Third, the need for persons everywhere to sheer away from the crass materialism of recent decades came through clearly. Many panelists seemed to feel that a surfeit of things (or "stuff") left a wide range of *psychological* and—if the times permit a vintage phrase—*spiritual* longings unsatisfied.

But, granting that just about everyone, at least on their own terms, is supportive of its goals—*what is moral education?* And how can the schools, as a major educational resource, help nourish an emerging moral dimension in U.S. life?

What one learns in school, according to John Dewey, is of moral value to the extent that this learning helps "the pupil sympathetically and imaginatively to appreciate the social scene [and] to realize his indebtedness to the great stream of human activities that flow thru [*sic*] and about him."[10]

Lawrence Kohlberg, known for his longitudinal research in moral development, also credits Dewey with early, important conjectures on the topic. Dewey suggested three levels of moral growth: (a) blind acceptance of instruction and admonition, (b) willing acceptance of the moral values of others, and (c) self-chosen moral directions. In this influential philosopher's view, moral virtue is not a miracle or an accident; it is the efficacious growth of the child's power to behave positively.[11] It is the application of insightful, self-chosen principles, principles of conscience that are in keeping with the Golden Rule.[12]

If this interpretation is acceptable to the reader, then it becomes possible to expand further the personalized learning center model to include the concept of the school as an important medium for fostering moral development (Component V—see Figure 11). Here, through careful, methodical instruction, the *very environment of the school* emerges as a *moral* force, if we define *moral* in broad terms:

---

[10] Professor Dewey's comment was made at a 1909 lecture before the Northern Illinois Teachers' Association in Elgin. Cited by George E. Axtelle and Joe R. Burnet, "Dewey on Education and Schooling," in Jo Ann Boydston, ed., *Guide to the Works of John Dewey.* Carbondale: Southern Illinois University Press, Arcturus Books Edition, 1972. p. 277.

[11] Dewey, *loc. cit.*

[12] For a concise statement of Lawrence Kohlberg's ideas regarding moral development, see his article, "The Cognitive-Developmental Approach to Moral Education," *Phi Delta Kappan* 56:670–677; June 1975.

FIGURE 11

The School
As a Personalized Learning Center *(concluded)*

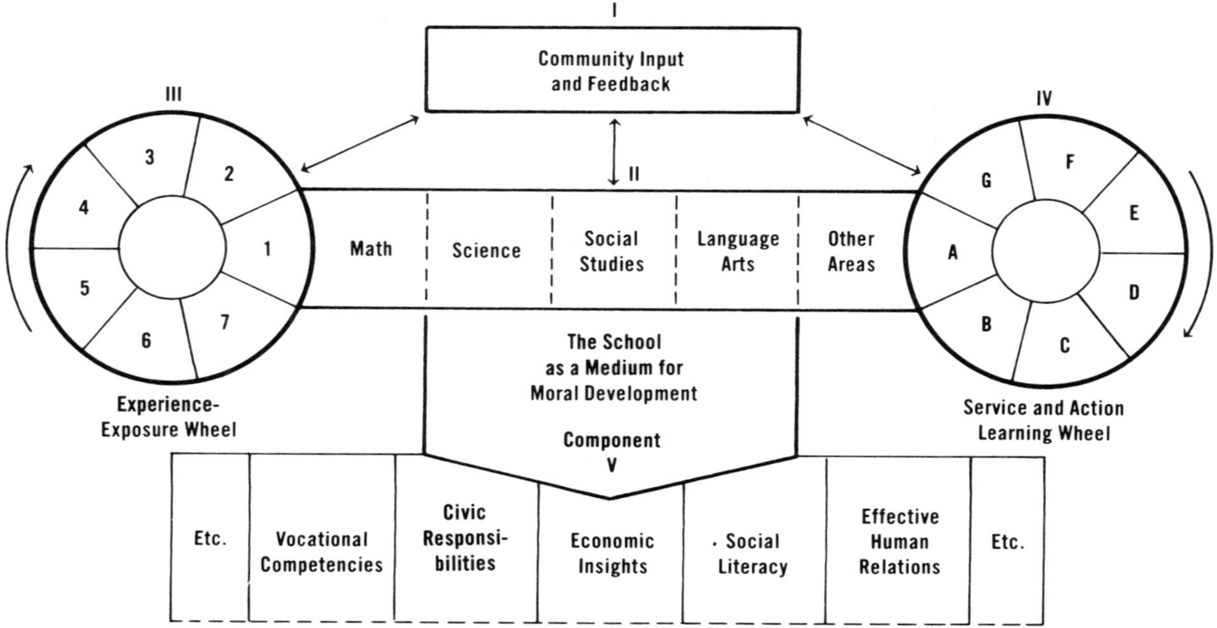

I — Community Input and Feedback

II — Math | Science | Social Studies | Language Arts | Other Areas

III — Experience-Exposure Wheel (1, 2, 3, 4, 5, 6, 7)

IV — Service and Action Learning Wheel (A, B, C, D, E, F, G)

V — The School as a Medium for Moral Development Component

Etc. | Vocational Competencies | Civic Responsibilities | Economic Insights | Social Literacy | Effective Human Relations | Etc.

1. *Vocational competencies* are stressed to make the learner useful to self and to society.
2. *Civic responsibilities* are emphasized as means of countering threats to freedom in a world where democratic nations are dwindling in number.
3. *Economic insights* are developed so as to delineate how resources can be used in moral ways which reflect prudent parsimony and fiscal common sense.
4. *Social literacy* is nourished so that an image of a good society surfaces in young learners' minds.
5. *Effective human relations* are fostered since it becomes "moral," as premise I suggests, "to develop a spirit of 'global community' in an increasingly interdependent world . . ." characterized by the mutual need and by dynamic reciprocity in resource sharing and in comparable practices that serve the general welfare.

And so on, as the "Etc." on the wings of the model is intended to suggest. Local discussion (or the seven cardinal goals!) will provide points in addition to the five listed in the model.

For both parents and classroom practitioners, there is an important concomitant question. If the school is conceived of as a personalized learning center that fosters personal-moral development and ethical character in addition to the nine areas of knowledge, just *how* is it done? What processes and procedures, what methods and materials are used, for example, to instill a sense of civic responsibility? Unfortunately, there seems no clear way to add a visual or graphic how-to-do-it component to the five components included in the model. Verbal images must suffice.

Two points seem especially significant at this juncture. First, the hidden curriculums—the valuing and value judgments of teachers—need to be examined by each teacher so that his or her language and demeanor provide a good human environment for the learner. How do they, as educators, react to the nine value dilemmas or moral issues itemized below—issues that confront most of us as we react to situations involving:

1. The role and nature of punishment
2. Property rights and obligations
3. The nature and role of love and affection
4. The role, duties, and limits of authority
5. The functions of law and enforcement
6. Sexual mores, pregnancy, and abortion

7. Liberty and the responsibilities of freedom
8. Justice and equity
9. Truth and the sacredness of a promise.[13]

Every teacher, almost each day, expresses a spectrum of moral values when reacting to situations involving the nine exemplars cited. The hidden or latent curriculum of values that a teacher projects or transmits is operating when a child is punished or when the teacher looks the other way to avoid seeing certain forms of pupil behavior; it is in the speech inflections of teachers and is mirrored in their body language; it manifests itself in reading lists and in the teachers' comments about their colleagues, politics, and world news events made within earshot of students.

We have noted that there are *two* points to be made with respect to fostering the development of ethical character. In addition to deliberate exploitation of the hidden curriculum for positive, socially worthy purposes, certain oft-neglected resources embedded in the structure of school life can be used to develop moral-ethical attitudes. *Moral-ethical* continues to refer to the interpretation these terms were given in Jonas Salk's tape. For a moral education, he indicated:

> We need to help children develop nobility. By "nobility" I mean doing the right thing for the right reason. I think this can be taught just as we teach arithmetic, reading, or biology.

Let us speculate about what can be done *in the school milieu* to help provide opportunities to learn what the *right thing* is and what the reasons are for honoring it. For one thing, teachers (and parents, as we repeatedly have indicated) are teaching moral values when they *themselves* are honest, open-minded, willing to admit an error, seek evidence rather than respond to rumor, are capable of acknowledging that they do not have all the answers, and are respectful of the promises they make—in fine, when they are exemplars of the best of the traditions of a polycultural American nation. The young will develop moral attitudes by contagion from adults who (by example rather than precept) distinguish between justice and tyranny, naked self-interest and humane behavior, honesty and guile—and help young learners to comprehend how to sort out the

---

[13]*Ibid.*, p. 672.

good from the evil. The hardest part of the trick is to learn how to do this without merely moralizing. Preachments may make youngsters aware of moral precepts, but they do not automatically assure ethical behavior.

Adult example, in itself, our speculations suggest, is not enough to nurture ethical character, however much it helps! Children and youth—indeed, all of us—need opportunities to *exercise* our ability to behave ethically. Here teachers and parents need to devise ways in which the school, a potential democracy in miniature, can serve as a kind of giant teaching aid in which and through which moral (just and equitable) values develop. Let us shift in our speculations from rhetoric to a few simple specific examples to illustrate this point.

Many schools, from the elementary years through postsecondary levels, have some form of student advisory councils. Often they accomplish little more than introducing pupils to the rudiments of civics or parliamentary procedures. Might it not be better, as a few schools have demonstrated, to have not a *student* council but a *school* council to which pupils *and teachers* are elected. Such an agency should have the prestige of responsibility and the power to legislate, within reasonable, prescribed limits, for the general welfare of the human community within the school. Real problems with ethical implications should provide grist for the council conceived here so that representatives in its assembly and its subcommittees can grapple with the moral issues appropriate to their ages and maturity. These problems can range from discussing and determining snowballing rules on an elementary school playground to such questions, at the university level, as mixed housing in campus dormitories.

Consider a second example. From the elementary school years onward, one usually finds bookstores selling what ranges from simple supplies at the primary level to the elaborate inventories of large universities. When such stores are located in elementary and secondary schools, they are likely to be managed by, say, a mathematics or business education teacher with the help of a few students. Why not, when possible, make the bookstore a student-run venture (with teacher advice)—perhaps a co-op? Many ethical decisions regarding pricing, the quality of products, the return of goods, dealing with suppliers, and, in a co-op, the return of profits to student investors, are involved.

In the same vein, a specialist in the field of occupational education recently described to the writer a project at the secondary level in which his shop class contracted to produce machined units for a local manufacturer. Again, a variety of ethical questions regarding price, quality, pay, and quotas from participating students provided a basis for ethical policy decisions.

An Illinois middle school developed an array of school- and community-sponsored activities, some 20 in all, which provided even more sophisticated experiences with ethical decision making.[14] To illustrate, youngsters in the cafeteria who received meals in return for dishwashing formed (with parent-teacher cooperation and direct help from a labor union representative) a dishwashers' union. The students bargained annually for a contract governing hours, compensation, responsibilities, and policies for such matters as china breakage. Since breakage was a major problem and issue, an insurance company was formed with the assistance of a local insurance man. Limited to cafeteria dish-breakage, the company developed printed policies, kept two adjusters in the lunch room, issued stock and, in the process had considerable experience, as Salk would put it, in doing the right thing for the right reason.

Other school ventures providing an opportunity to think and act ethically can be imagined: sitter services under school auspices, a school loan office with a $5 ceiling run (and financed by) young adolescents, and minicorporations that raise and sell plants for profit or keep bees and harvest the honey for sale.

But the point already should have been made. The young, on whom so many key social decisions of the 1980's and long thereafter will depend, learn what they live. They are governed by what their parents, teachers, and other adults *do,* not by what they *say.* Furthermore, young people often are quick to spot hypocritical statements and adult phonies. By our behavior as teachers and as parents, we best can educate for a new millennium through moral educational practices and character development. This is accomplished not only through our example but by experiences, such as

---

[14]Each activity, such as the small-scale union described, was sponsored by a faculty member. The young people held periodic business meetings, and their work involved profit-making and income—an aspect of the ventures which lent a great deal of meaning to pupil decision making and the ethics involved therein. Groups were chartered by an elected pupil-teacher school council.

those mentioned, in guided ethical decision making in real situations which good, imaginative schooling can provide. These should be varied, challenging, truly involve children and youth, and be considered an integral part of the educative process.

SUMMARY.   Chapter IX, in dealing with the school as a personalized learning center, emphasized the importance of close school and community rapport, the importance of substantive content and of additional skills that have become basic for life in a world in rapid transition. The idea that the school should provide exposure experiences was introduced, and the importance of learning actively through service was strongly endorsed, thus recognizing the NEA panelists' strong opinions in this regard.

Finally, the subtle nature of moral values and of ethical character development was presented so as to stress the importance of having repeated and personalized experiences which require direct involvement as well as participation by the young in the invariably demanding task of doing right for the right reason at their individual level of comprehension. This is a supremely important reason for conceiving the school as a center for personalized, wholesome human growth and a quality of living that leads to a responsible and responsive maturity.

EPILOGUE

As I look back on the 14 months invested in the present project and to the opportunity these months have provided for work with bright, interesting, and dedicated members of the human community, I find that the experiences I have had have had a profound influence on my own viewpoints and attitudes.

For instance, my respect for the power and the versatility of the human mind has increased and my belief in the greatness and kindness of people—with a few rare exceptions—has been reaffirmed.

At the same time it has been brought home to me in much greater detail the truly frightful problems that will beset humankind during the years immediately ahead. I have also become much more aware of the need for portentous, rapid decisions which these problems will demand. Yet while our time is short in which to bring order out of the crisis of crises, it seems entirely probable that the ability of men and women of good will is great enough, if they combine forces everywhere, to defuse our crises in the next 20 years.

There seems reason to disagree vehemently with those who feel that our long roster of troubles betokens the decline of our species. The challenges which we must meet are not the signs of our decline. Rather, they are the result of our rapid rise from the savagery of the cave to the complex interdependence and mutual need which have come to characterize twentieth century living.

Whether or not our educational agencies will have the vision and the power needed to create educational changes not just for a new century but for life in a new millennium is a moot question. Hopefully, however, by the year 2001 A.D. we will have verified the hope that the fundamental problems now facing us are occurring in the dusk before cockcrow rather than in the gathering gloom of a long twilight.

APPENDIX A
TESTIMONY OF THE TAPES

The following excerpts are taken from the taped interviews conducted for the NEA Project to reframe the seven cardinal principles and develop curriculum guidelines for a new millennium. With a few exceptions, excerpts from the interviews that were quoted in the body of the text are not repeated here. Also, a variety of different excerpts were selected in order to minimize the repetition of similar points made by many of the panelists.

KEY TO TAPED EXCERPTS. The names of all the NEA International Panel members and several of the Project Pre-Planning Committee members are indexed below to help the reader identify specific statements.

[1]Affiliations given are those at the time of the NEA Bicentennial Project.

---

[1]Affiliations given are those at the time of the NEA Bicentennial Project.

Name of participant	Affiliation[1]	Page
Smilansky, Moshe	University of Tel Aviv	154
Smith, B. Othanel	University of Illinois (Emeritus) and University of South Florida (Emeritus) (Pre-Planning Committee)	155
Tanaka, Paul	Tacoma (Washington) Association of Classroom Teachers	155
Terkel, Louis (Studs)	Chicago radio commentator	156
Thompson, John M.	World Confederation of Organizations of the Teaching Profession	156
Tyler, Ralph W.	Center for Advanced Study in the Behavioral Sciences (Emeritus), Stanford	156
Wedgeworth, Robert, Jr.	American Library Association	158
Wise, Helen D.	Pennsylvania teacher; former NEA president	158

Amara, Roy:

If I were to select the single feature characterizing this period, it would be *change,* and the second prominent feature is *complexity.*

One of our crucial tasks is how to define and to operationalize the definition of equity.

Education must support active and direct participation in self-government, for only through such participation can a complex society achieve its social goals.

We might well return to the notion of apprenticeship with interwoven periods of work and formal schooling.

Baisinger, Grace C.:

Frankly, I feel like I am an immigrant in my own world. It is certainly not the one I was born into.

Tension in the future probably will develop along economic rather than ethnic lines unless it is forestalled by careful planning to reduce the discrepancy between haves and have-nots.

Some forms of learning may be less important in the 21st century.

---

[1]Affiliations given are those at the time of the NEA Bicentennial Project.

Emphasis may be on how to use the sources of knowledge rather than on memorization.

As ways are found to wed computers to library resource centers, I see libraries becoming more important to the educational process. Possibly the role of conventional schooling will diminish.

We should think in terms of forward to the basics rather than back to the basics. The new basics will include the attainment of decision-making skills and skills in human relationships.

I see the nuclear family surviving along with a variety of other lifestyles that will come to be accepted.

As the world grows smaller we must not retain a narrow, chauvinistic meaning of citizenship.

Benevidez, Patricia:

A challenge for the schools is to move toward values clarification. We need to continue opening up alternatives at the grassroots level.

Blakeslee, Donald:

I see the seven cardinal principles becoming skills for survival.

The burning issue is, What happens when my leisure thing gets in the way of your leisure thing.

Some wonder why students have to use vulgar words. I see the use of four-letter words as part of a quest for honesty.

One of the most significant things in my lifetime was to see the view of the Earth from the Moon.

So far as the three R's are concerned, if you want to strike out "writin' " and put in "relatin' " it's o.k. with me.

Blanchard, François:

Concue comme il vient d'être dit, la liberté suppose le respect des différences et du droit de les exprimer; langues et cultures régionales et nationales; moeurs, coutumes, philosophies, religions.

Mais il existe manifestement des traits généraux communs au moins à tous les pays qui ont atteint un certain degré de développement économique.

La maîtrise des moyens d'expression—langue maternelle et autres—joue un role primordial pour l'acquisition des connaissances et l'aptitude a la communication entre hommes.

Une éducation civique, démocratique et humaniste doit non seulement donner aux élèves une large information (économique, politique, morale, sexuelle) mais également les initier au debat critique et à l'exercise de responsabilités dans l'établissement scolaire.

Bloom, Benjamin:

Educated persons must be more than doctors, engineers, or scientists; they must be effective citizens and human beings.

The world's hierarchical societies are ending; a common man's society is surfacing.

We are going to develop a world view rather than a national view.

Education should not be sought for its economic payoff so much as for the kind of life it facilitates.

Work and leisure will become less dichotomized as we see more clearly the meaning of a fulfilling life. . . .

About 94 percent of our "slower" learners, if we take more time with them, can reach the achievement level of "fast" ones.

Teachers will become models of humans relating to humans, not merely persons skilled in a content field.

Taking ideas and relating them in novel situations is the command of fundamental process.

In the future, vocational competency will be acquired more often outside of school, and the school will focus on the general knowledge required by all vocations. . . .

In the years ahead the *examined* life rather than the *good* life will be an educational goal. . . .

Worthy home membership involves doing what one can for the coming generation.

Boulding, Elise:

It is important in the teaching–learning process to engage people from all the different subcultures.

I see in 1996 a low or intermediate technology for the way we live; high technology for the way we communicate.

The seven cardinal principles should become cardinal principles for *lifelong* learning experiences. It's not just what education can do for the young. If at age 65 you want a new set of skills, you should be able to enter the same network. It's one network for everyone.

The more we talk about competency-based education, the less competent people feel.

There's nothing wrong with any of the cardinal principles as long as we think of them as goals for the total community education process.

The things which make us a good member of the *family* are the same skills that we bring to successful *community* living.

Bowser, Vivian:

I recognize that we need to accept the reality of interdependence, but I think this should be built on a base of independence.

We unrealistically isolate and block off boys and girls into age groups we call grades. These fragment our efforts and our educational balance.

We will either develop basic skills more adequately or our ignorance will annihilate us.

Brewton, Agnes:

I foresee educational complexes in the inner city which respond to many kinds of interests; some in education, others focusing on fundamentals, on multicultural heritages, on college preparatory, or on vocational education.

Many teachers have strong positive feelings about increased emphasis on the basic skills of the traditional school.

Brown, Lester R.:

We are crossing the threshold of a great discontinuity in human history. . . .

Some of our old concepts of success have actually become a threat to our survival in an increasingly crowded world.

Industrialization and technology, affluence and growth were emphasized in the past; but we are now pressing against the borders of a finite world and this new reality will profoundly shape the future. . . .

The ecological information that most adults have today was not obtained from their schooling but from the communications media.

Formal and traditional forms of schooling [in the next 20 years] will not play as big a role as in the past. Humankind must reach fundamental decisions before most children now in our schools can participate in the decision-making process. . . .

Rugged individualism and resource depletion simply are irreconcilable. A society that doesn't discipline itself in the use of its resources in the foreseeable future will be forced into regulation and the loss of many freedoms.

The nuclear family will not be the universal building block in the future that it has been in the past. In some cities unattached individuals and childless couples, married and unmarried, now outnumber conventional families.

"Health" now means that the young must have a knowledge of faulty U.S. life-styles; that overconsumption can be as debilitating as underconsumption; that 60 to 90 percent of all cancer is caused by environmental factors such as air pollution. . . .

Vocational efficiency transcends skill training. It also emphasizes competence in such abilities as problem solving. We need to develop a new breed of vocationally competent persons who see not just how to do something but its implications for the ecosystem.

It will become increasingly difficult to separate work and leisure in the years ahead. I don't know, for instance, when I'm in the garden plot whether I am doing work or engaging in a leisure-time activity. It remains to be seen whether, between 1966 and 1996, the formal

U.S. educational system can teach survival behaviors. If it succeeds, it will be by establishing a new conception of lifelong, continuing education. In the process, teachers constantly must be re-educated and curricula constantly updated and renewed.

World citizenship means thinking about the kind of world we seek and tackling such problems as resource sharing and working for [anti-] hijacking treaties.

Bundy, McGeorge:

Trends can be identified. However, we probably will have continued acceleration in our accumulation of knowledge, and knowledge will be more closely interconnected.

As far as the worthy use of leisure is concerned, I think there is going to be a trend toward spending more time making or growing what people used to buy in the marketplace.

Education will be increasingly concerned with *how* to learn.

What we need to know probably will be more carefully selected because of the total amount available to be learned.

Effective citizenship and vocational efficiency are more complex today because life is more complex.

Castro, Raul H.:

The majority language of America, and of much of the world's business, is English. This makes bilingual education a top priority in our country to make certain that all people will be able to communicate fluently, and not be shut out of the mainstream of our society. . . .

Widespread education is one of the glories and assets of our nation, but there are more marked variations in the quality of education [in the U.S.] than among most other advanced nations. The gap between a poor school in a depressed area and a good school in an affluent area in enormous. Our great universities are unmatched anywhere. But there is also a legion of colleges in which standards are low and facilities inadequate. We like to think of education as the great equalizer, offering all students equal opportunity. But a look at some of our schools shows that some schools are more equal than others. The pretense that physical environment is unimportant simply evades this most basic issue. We must find answers for these disparities in the future.

If we cannot always bring the children of migrant workers to our schools on a regular basis, then the challenge is to find appropriate means to bring education to these children. We must remember that the secret of education lies in respecting the pupil, which must include not only those pupils in regular classrooms, but also those who may rarely see the inside of a classroom.

I think we should add equality as the eighth cardinal principle of education, thus giving this fundamental human right a separate and distinct emphasis of its own. I recognize that equality is certainly an integral part of the original seven principles but I believe it needs an individual consideration in order to receive full and just emphasis in the future.

Clementi, Nick:

We need greater realism in school. Far too often students are given an idealistic view.

We should give students the opportunity to obtain basic skills at an early age. As soon as they can govern themselves, they should be given freedom to choose among alternatives.

Cohen, Wilbur J.:

With a much larger, older population in 2000, we've a potential problem on our hands with regard to establishing a much better system of communication between older and younger generations.

The educational system 25 years hence will be financed more adequately from a combination of full employment and the probability that there will not be any substantial increase . . . in fertility rates.

How to obtain participation other than in elections is a key problem of a democratic society.

By the year 2000, I think we will have in place a national minimum income guarantee system . . . as well as a government commitment to full employment.

Mandatory special education for every child up until the age of 25 will become an accepted characteristic of the educational system.

We will have, by the year 2000, a comprehensive national health plan that will make it possible for every child that is born to develop with a maximum opportunity for good health.

Conover, Hobart H.:

Technological advances will permit more education in the home and outside the walls of formal school settings.

Human drives, motivation, leadership capabilities, and skill in working as a productive member of a group should be emphasized.

The seven cardinal principles reflect a narrower and more circumspect society than we're likely to encounter in the 21st century.

In the future we will see more emphasis on career guidance to reduce unrest, dissatisfaction, and dislike of work.

Cousins, Norman:

The reach of my education was limited to the Western world and as a result I graduated from college only half educated.

Since human nature is always changing, one of the purposes of education is to see that it changes for the better.

An essential problem for education is helping people learn how to deal with acceleration, to comprehend more complex relationships, and to anticipate probable developments in the future.

Education also must contribute to our development of *collective* human intelligence—how we can bring intellectual candle power to illuminate our problems.

There are only two "political parties" in the world today, those humans who are sensitized and those who have become desensitized.

The human prospect if we win is beyond all imagining. We can draw energy from that prospect, if we turn our eyes to the future and penetrate the present despair. Beyond the despair we have credentials for survival that haven't begun to be enumerated.

Survival has always been the automatic test of a successful education.

Computers cannot be programmed to deal with the great problems and imponderables of history. Computers can't be programmed with a mind like those of Buckminster Fuller or Thomas Jefferson nor can they be programmed to anticipate a windfall.

It is fundamental that we know how to weight and sort information, to find unifying factors.

The seven cardinal principles are as valid as ever but their world context is now very different.

Health education also should help the young to learn that society is losing its oxygen; that skies are becoming open sewers; that the seas are dumping grounds in which marine life finds it difficult to survive.

It is important to remember that there may be disintegrative forces eroding children and youth, forces which the schools cannot by themselves adequately counter.

An objective of the goal of health is to help us to cope with stress and stress points, to recognize that many of our stress problems are interwoven with unwise life-styles.

The command of fundamental processes involves the ability to make correlations and to see the connections between things.

The school is sometimes faced with the melancholy necessity of trying to do the job of both home and school.

We must try to understand what is happening so that we can go on to try to do new things for the first time.

Cremin, Lawrence A.:

Scrutinize where things are learned and ask: (1) Where can they best be learned? and (2) When we decide where to teach them, keep in mind that they may have been taught elsewhere, correctly or incorrectly.

By the year 2000 the organized community may decide it wants to do more things over television than in the public schools.

We need to teach people to learn all the forms of communication that they can learn. And we need to teach them to be critical of communication as one way of developing control over the use of that communication as when we teach people to read, we teach them the arts of literary criticism so that they do not become the victims of what they read.

An important issue is, Where can any given thing that needs to be taught best be learned? It is a way of looking "ecologically" at education.

To list the command of fundamental processes with the other six goals of education is like mixing apples and peaches.

We need to make sure that there is not one committee of teachers sitting down somewhere making social goals for the school system and talking in terms of global concepts such as world citizenship while another committee of teachers is busy reorganizing the individual subjects. The trouble in our time is that the two kinds of committees have failed to meet.

Dror, Yehezkel:

Various changes in technology and in life-styles do not make too much difference in the *qualitative* contents of education and its challenges.

In the future it will be more important than ever that individuals be equipped with the individual capacity to make value-explicit choices based on information on the one hand and to think creatively on the other hand.

The basic problems of the 21st century will not be very different: conflicting ideologies reinforced by devastating and relatively cheap weapon systems; tensions between different social groups; and most important of all, the fundamental problems of the meanings of life and the purposes of existence.

Ellena, William:

We need to identify "educational imperatives" for the next two decades.

Elm, Lloyd:

We are in a period of rapid social evolution. I reject the melting-pot concept through education; there are too many unmelted lumps left in the pot.

We [native Americans] see the educational process, as it is now, as an instrument of cultural genocide.

European-Americans have cultures to return to. The native American has no foreign land to which he can return to verify his heritage.

I hope that by 2000 A.D. education is going to be a multiethnic process from which each of us profits from the best of the culture of the other.

Health, and I mean mental health, must include self-esteem if it is to be attained.

A fundamental process today [for native Americans] is education for cultural survival.

To develop citizenship skills a child must grow up in a country with a government he can respect.

The meaning of ethical character, which governs the other six cardinal objectives, should be reflected in the way we practice ethical behavior—for instance, as reflected in our respecting the ecological relationship.

Forbes, Jack:

We may have a world in which the average government is fascist or communist dictatorship.

Some goals of education which native Americans think are important include first, the goal of maximum development of individual spiritual potential and second, maintenance or re-establishment of "community" leading to a nonexploitive harmony with one's environment.

An old Delaware Indian teacher said, "When one meditates on good, it causes one to be good."

There's been too much of a movement to explore the future without enough effort to understand our own past.

Foy, Joe H.:

I see no relief in this century where the energy problem is concerned.

I am concerned about the availability of capital between now and the year 2000. This could cause trouble in the business community because substantial funds are needed for developing sources of energy.

I anticipate more government regulation, continued and expanded welfare provisions, and a proliferation of big government.

As our gas reserves go down we must place reater reliance on coal. We will continue to be dependent on Middle East oil for many years to come.

Our heroes and heroines of history should be presented accurately and honestly but there is nothing to be gained from denigrating them so ruthlessly that we make cynics of our youth.

One of the things I would say is most important is teaching young people how to detect and to avoid ambiguity in the language they use. Communication is the most vital of the learned processes.

Regarding the seven cardinal principles of education, I wouldn't change a one of them.

Teaching suffered in the 1960's and early 1970's because of the turbulence on campuses. The turbulence received the attention at a loss to education. Educational leadership at all levels should concentrate on making up the academic time losses during the last 15 years.

With reference to vocational education, some persons' ambitions outrun both their ability and their command of fundamental processes.

Harman, Willis W.:

We need to learn to be loyal to our planet as well as to our family, our state, and our nation.

Each generation is born on a different planet because changes occur so quickly.

We have separated out too many things that used to be together and should be together—leisure, religion, and vocation.

During the next 20 years the legitimacy of the social system of the industrial, technological world will be seriously challenged.

The importance of *education* is crucial during the next 20 years, but the criticality of *schooling* is questionable because young people now in school will still be too young to participate in decisions that must be reached before irreparable damage is done to the biosphere.

We are wrestling everywhere with a moral-principles crisis because of the problems immediately ahead of us.

Education should be characterized by mutual learning by teachers and pupils, not merely the transmitting of information from teachers to pupils.

There are so many problems for which we don't have answers that teachers and students need to grope their way together toward a future that neither has yet comprehended.

We need a "process curriculum" in which teacher and student quest together.

Once we had generations in which to respond to problems. Now on many of these problems we have at most a single generation in which to think, to decide, and to act.

The three R's retain their importance as "fundamentals" but it is also fundamental for us to develop evaluation skills in an era of information glut and when so many things need to be sorted out.

We shouldn't look for a substitute for the family; we should strive to alter the forces that serve to destroy it.

There probably always will be a need for a small community of intimates but not necessarily blood-related. I think that the family, because of our need for intimates, is staging a comeback but it won't be easy.

Havighurst, Robert J.:

The seven cardinal principles provide a useful taxonomy, but some of the original interpretations now seen naive in retrospect.

We will need to move toward planetary citizenship.

We must learn to create as much as we use. We should think of ourselves as trustees rather than owners of the world's treasurers.

"Ethical character" can't be developed on a relativistic base. . . . The meaning of personal morality must be clarified between 1976 and 2001; moral codes need to be re-examined and reaffirmed.

One of our challenges is to develop the concept of human geography.

We must learn what to do in order to maintain individual freedom and self-determination in a more tightly regulated society.

Worthy family membership should involve a five-generation model—from grandparents to great grandchildren.

Remember that the children of 2050 will be just as valuable as our children are now.

We must tool up *now* if we want to be ready for the year 2001.

Hesburgh, Theodore M.:

Among educational imperatives needed are greater flexibility in teaching and learning, education for a dynamic world, and nurturing of intellectual curiosity so that there will be a yearning to keep on learning.

The enormous growth in human knowledge will continue to complicate the educational task.

We have today an inequitable and unjust world order and the gap presently is widening between those who have and those who lack. There must be some sort of redress possible for persons in the third and fourth world[s].

. . . it is almost obscene, the way so many millions of Americans are overfed. It is unreasonable for a small part of the world to think of heart transplants while the rest doesn't see a doctor from birth to death.

We must not merely try to redistribute the pie of the "have" nations. We must enlarge the pie so that the disenfranchised have a greater share. We must play a game where everyone wins.

We have gone overboard with our monstrous cars, our waste of food and our consumption of raw materials. Someone has said that the world couldn't stand two Americas; I am not sure it can stand one!

I anticipate an ecumenical spirit characterized by greater understanding and increased appreciation of things in life that we value.

To be effective overseas, we must first develop a strong sense of citizenship and responsibility at home.

A greater sense of moral responsibility needs to be restored. Too much of it has been filtered out in a highly secularized society. Too many young people today think that morals are established by taking a poll. This is ridiculous. It suggests that there are no standards, that everything is relative.

I see more changing life-styles ahead for our country because of the struggle between the spiritual and the material. No nation can be great if it is merely given over to materialism.

We continue to need the discipline of wrestling with ideas that appear in print. Books permit you to select while TV selects for you.

Vocational education must not lock people into jobs—jobs that may not exist in the years ahead.

Education should introduce children to the use of leisure time for service. Leisure without opportunities for growth and service simply results in boredom.

Jarvis, Fred:

"Interdependence," in my view, means the development not just of a collective society, but of a collectivist world. There is no other way of coping with the pressure on our planet's resources and meeting the needs of our common humanity.

At least for a few years, even the inadequate provisions we now have for [British] education are going to be cut because of the economic situation. . . . We are going to the barricades to defend what we have.

Decisions about the future content of education [in Great Britain] are being made without any formal or official attempt to picture society as it is going to be 10, 20, 30 years hence. There is no body or source in our education system indulging in futurology. Largely, we depend on the judgment of the teaching profession.

We have got to recognize that the individual, when he leaves school, has to earn a living. He can't just be educated in an "ivory tower" sense.

We're giving attention now to the transition from school to work, equipping the individual for life in industry as well as social and family living.

You cannot demand rights for involvement in decision making without recognizing the responsibilities that go with it.

The freedom which the individual school enjoys in our education system places great responsibility on the [teaching] profession.

Johnson, John H.:

Leisure? Most blacks don't have it!

There will be a redistribution of power both in the U.S. and between the U.S. and the developing world.

Don't assume that education *per se* eliminates prejudice and discrimination. The educated person often has more plausible reasons for discriminating. I would rather deal with an uneducated man than an educated one if both were prejudiced.

Basically, the cardinal principles are good, but some need to be extended and modernized.

Greater economic power for blacks will help keep families together.

The vocational preparation of blacks should include accounting, operating computers, mathematics, engineering, and other skills of a technological society.

Participation skills and the positive use of power are part of civic competence.

Children need to learn that we believe and trust them if they are to develop ethical character.

Laidlaw, John, Jr.:

One of our educational tasks will be that of preserving the freedom we are honoring at the Bicentennial.

Our list of problems keeps getting longer while our time to overcome them is getting shorter.

Nowadays "health education" is much broader than it was in 1918. It runs through family living, it includes coping with drug abuse, and understanding how your body works.

Lear, Norman:

I feel like we're all strapped together on a toboggan, going down a steep slope, and with a giant tree in the way. And we've got to steer clear of it.

We've got to find the kind of leadership that won't abdicate responsibility while leading. People want more than to be polled. They also want to be told.

I'm the original optimist, like the twin playing happily in the manure who said, "With all this s--- around, there's got to be a pony someplace."

I've too often seen my children poured through the same little funnel with the rest of the class so they all sound the same.

There is no substitute for reading. It is just as important as it ever was.

I would wish my grandchildren to be taught one thing early, and that is that people are basically good.

It is the duty of education to teach that people are good and that the individual matters.

When I think of my daughters, I'm immediately obsessed with the thought, Will there be a world in which they can live out their marvelous young fantasies?

Nothing is more important than for children to be taught that they matter. As individuals, they *do* matter. All education should begin with that.

Mackenzie, Malcolm:

I think there is a danger of oversimplistic interpretations of the idea that we don't need schools at all. But I think what is necessary is the more efficient management of schools, a greater understanding of the relationship of schools to societies.

In a changing world it's extremely difficult to know what is "fundamental."

The schools always have a problem in handling areas of political controversy.

The problem in a changing society is to know what vocations are going to be required in 10 or 15 years.

If democracy is to survive and spread, then people are going to have to be more sophisticated in decision making.

McMurrin, Sterling:

The future will be marked by automation, mechanization, cybernation, and certainly by an increase in bureaucracy. All of this, I am afraid, adds up to a great threat to individuality and personality.

We are past the stage where we can assume that in some way it's possible to get by on anything like the British capacity to muddle through.

Concern for the individual is really the genius of our culture.

Except for literacy and possibly vocational efficiency, the cardinal objectives of education as traditionally stated are tasks of the total society, not simply of the schools. The primary and defining task of a school is, or ought to be, its commitment to knowledge and to the cultivation of reason. A school is properly concerned with the qualities of reasonableness.

Missing from the cardinal principles are references to the aesthetic experience, to art and beauty; that is a very serious omission and should be corrected.

Mink, Patsy Takemoto:

The average citizen today neither fathoms nor is receptive to the changes that are occurring in other lands. Antagonism easily results from this kind of ignorance.

It is important for American education to help young people make a much more honest appraisal of the American condition in relation to other countries. The young need to have a deeper and more intense appreciation for the politics in other countries. Much of the rest of the world is only mentioned in passing during the years of a child's school experience. This is not only unrealistic but probably damaging to the national character.

You don't go to school any more just to learn to brush your teeth. Keeping well also means learning how to cope with physically harmful qualities in the environment.

I belong to the old-fashioned school that believes in mastery of basics. Educational theory has swung too far away from practices that focus on Johnny's ability to read. We must keep our allegiance to a high level of literacy for all.

Ethical character involves a regard for other people and education should develop a sense of responsibility for others.

Nieto, Consuelo:

It is becoming even more important to provide students with real bilinguality, biliteracy, biculturalism, and to help them sense that these dimensions give strength to our nation.

Home—if it ever was—certainly is no longer that little white house with "Spot" and Mother and Father and Dick and Jane and the white picket fence.

The three R's need to be integrated with the affective domain.

The NEA must be more than a union—more than salary and working conditions. The Association must provide teachers with resources for dealing with students' needs.

Passow, A. Harry:

In an interdependent world we must concentrate on clarifying our values and resolving our conflicts.

If we extricate ourselves from our current problems, life will be very different 25 years hence from what it is now.

It is educationally imperative for us to replace rote learning with higher thought processes and problem solving. We also must face real-life issues in school and do what we can to end pressure for conformity.

We need to know how to keep well in a carcinogenic and cardiac society. This means greater stress must be placed on mental as well as physical health.

Child rearing differs very much today from the practices of even 30 years ago. Male and female roles have changed so greatly that what was "good" in 1918 may very well be "bad" child-rearing practice today.

Much that has been done in secondary education in the name of developing vocational skill might better have been accomplished outside the school.

Strong general education is needed for the development of vocational competence.

As far as civic education goes, education must now place emphasis on membership in a much larger society.

It seems to me that it is a question of whether anyone will have much leisure by the time most people get through moonlighting to combat inflation.

Perry, Sir Walter:

We are at a crisis point in human history. Society as we have known it may break down for a number of reasons. . . .

We must be sure that technology does not become the ultimate tyranny, but I do not see the human spirit accepting that subjugation.

A crucial trend is already discernible—a trend that, unfortunately, is not toward equality of opportunity, but toward unearned equality. In Britain some people no longer seek to improve themselves but to pull others down to their level.

Education should lead one out from inside himself.

We must get away from the idea that *all* education occurs in the early years of life. Continuing learning throughout life must be the rule. Initial education is far too long and much too fragmented. . . .

Our young people want a voice in decision making that affects them.

Too many scholars train their students in their own image rather than for effective living as mature human beings. . . .

Participation skills are important to self-realization; therefore, preparation for [participation] is just as important as vocational education.

All of the seven cardinal principles could be subsumed under two: (1) vocational efficiency and (2) self-fulfillment. "Self-fulfillment" is the ability of an individual to respond to the needs life imposes for ethical character, responsible parenthood, and the like.

At least for a year or two during their schooling, I would turn young people at 16 or 18 into the world to do useful work. . . .

By the time they finish [advanced degrees], many graduate students are so old that they lack drive; much of their information also may be obsolete or unnecessary. . . .

Too many scientists are numerate but not literate. . . .

Pierce, Wendell:

We must be mindful of the fact that there are different ethical systems in the world or else we will be constantly in conflict with persons from other nations with regard to what is "good" and what is "just."

Other agencies must be included in the total task of education.

As far as skill development is concerned, I don't think anyone in his right mind is in favor of any form of illiteracy that we can avoid.

As far as effective citizenship is concerned, we are still teaching the "surface stuff."

Ray, Doris:

Obviously we are going to be concerned about vocational efficiency, but I think we'll find that the schools as such will not necessarily be preparing for jobs *per se* as they were thought to do back in the early 20th century.

Basic literacy skills are essential, but the redefinition of what "fundamental processes" are should include such things as problem solving, expansion of communication skills, and extension of fundamental processes.

Teachers will become planners, coordinators of information and resources—a new type of teacher-model.

Rockefeller, David:

The pace of change seems likely to increase and the impact of technology on our institutions including schools will continue to be great at all levels.

The value of forecasts resides in the way they call our attention to problems that previously had not been detected or had not been clearly or adequately perceived.

My own feeling is that people who would limit growth fail to take into account that to diminish poverty—to improve the life of billions of people living at a bare subsistence level—we *have* to have continued growth.

Education should stress the need to work out a balance or create a state of equilibrium between our present situation and a more equitable sharing of the world's goods. But we also need to increase our efficiency in producing them. Up to now sharing and producing haven't moved hand in hand. If we seek equity without effectively increasing production, we will simply end up by redistributing poverty.

A Club-of-Rome-type report can't really probe the limits to growth because there is no way for their projections to allow for the adaptability of humans. The validity of their conclusions depends entirely on the data that were used in the first place.

The suggestion that we have reached the limits of growth has been picked up by a number of people who would rather like to see growth limited. If they can find allegedly "scientific" excuses to stop growth, they make every use of it.

Media other than schools are likely to be of increasing importance on the educational scene.

We do need, in the future, to be more careful in our use of resources and in our selection of priorities—but I don't believe it means that we have to stop growing. If, for instance, we do not have growth in finding new sources of energy, the result will have a devastating effect on standards of living throughout the world.

Everything does not have to be learned from scratch. I think that young people need to be familiar with the blueprints for the wheel when they seek to design one that will work more efficiently. They don't start by trying to reinvent the wheel.

The seven cardinal principles are fine—completely valid—but only if we interpret them in the context of the future rather than in their past setting.

The many changes in contemporary life lead to a need to emphasize a liberal education with stress on the survival skills demanded by the real world.

If it is to stand the test of time, democracy requires that the young learn about our democratic traditions and the policies they lead us to support.

Rumberger, Dale:

It is difficult to reconcile the problem of accountability and the need for accurate feedback with the need to impart the feeling that one can control one's own destiny.

College will become more of a "forum of thought," not a place for the regurgitation of knowledge . . . just one step below "think tanks."

It's difficult for me to rule out nuclear war . . . I see us coming very close, or actually having one.

Salk, Jonas:

We still have a great deal to learn about the nature of human beings—their needs and of how the mind and body work. Education can develop only as rapidly as we develop these insights.

We must endeavor to help children understand and to equip children with the understanding that we must think about increased cooperation rather than an increase in our competitive behavior.

Schools need to find ways of introducing the dynamic concept of how one can anticipate change.

We must consider health in two categories: biological health and metabiological health.

We need to help children develop nobility. By "nobility" I mean doing the right thing for the right reason. I think this can be taught just as we teach arithmetic or reading or biology.

Shelley, Sally Swing:

A global, nuclear war could so damage our ecological balance as to make life on the planet impossible. We must all understand that nuclear war is impossible.

The shape of the future depends on how we respond to it. One of our responses will depend upon our success in teaching the reality of our global interdependence.

What happens in one corner of the globe has repercussions everywhere.

Toy soldiers should always be dressed in 19th century uniforms or medieval armor since war is no longer an option.

The highest goal of health education is peace because we won't survive very long without it.

I would prefer to change the "worthy use of leisure time" to the "creative use of leisure time."

"Ethical character" involves a respect for human intelligence that will enable humankind to create a 21st century world in which people share with one another their respect, friendship, and prudence in conserving resources.

Sipilä, Helvi:

I can say that unless we take seriously the fate of women in developing countries, I don't think we can solve many of the other problems in the world: population, food shortage, illiteracy, abandoned children, unemployment, and mass poverty. . . .

We must close the gap that now exists between the developed and developing countries.

In developing countries, to their own disadvantage, they have adopted too much of the educational systems of the colonial countries and of the formal Western system of schooling. What the people of the developing world really need is rapid training for what is needed for the immediate improvement of their own economic and social status.

Sizer, Theodore R.:

The [NEA] project will be the poetry of informed opinion rather than hard research.

Individual schools try to take on too many tasks at once. . . . We may do a far better job as schoolmen by lowering our sights—paradoxical as that might sound.

Smilansky, Moshe:

We cannot plan, except according to our values.

The main responsibilities of the universities in the future, with the type of manpower that they have, with the type of students that are going through them, is to develop interconnecting regional support systems.

The focus of schooling will be on self-development and coping and problem solving through participatory democracy.

Many school reforms did not produce what was expected because the assumption was that the problem is for someone to develop a blueprint, and to distribute this blueprint among teachers who would adapt to it.

When I say planning, I mean *not* the statistical projections, not the forecasts with the assumptions that what was yesterday may be tomorrow with certain changes. It's the confrontation of the options that are available to us potentially. It's the opening of new options.

We have the option of influencing both the tempo and mode of the modernization process in our own life and in the life of our children.

Smith, B. Othanel:

The world must learn to move from irrational to rational behavior, from force to persuasion, from laissez faire to planning, from international anarchy to world order.

Tanaka, Paul:

Our resolution of human differences will not take place in a melting pot. Instead we must think of the example of a mosaic pattern or stained glass window in which all the pieces fit together while individual identity is preserved.

Bilingual education needs emphasis. There are many situations and there will be more in the future where one man who speaks two languages is worth two men.

We must recognize that there are 5 million children in the United States whose first languages are not English.

Terkel, Louis (Studs):

. . . work without meaning makes life equally meaningless.

The Protestant work ethic should be replaced by a social ethic which, paradoxically, will bring new and wholesome meaning to the work ethic.

Too many schools simply teach our young people how to "make it" at someone else's expense.

Thompson, John M.:

The world will remain a place of intense competition at the level of individuals, groups, classes, societies, civilizations, and nations.

The fundamental question is whether human ingenuity has reached its limit.

Tyler, Ralph W.:

The increasing economic well-being of organized groups is taking place to the detriment of children, youth, the unemployed, and older people, who are not an active part of the economy.

There is no biological difference between children born 200 years ago and those born today, except today's child probably is heavier and healthier. They're just the same kids. The difference is that the present demands so much more learning of the young. This requires us to look at the total learning system and not just the component we call schools.

We must face the problem of providing a broader structure of experience than the school now provides.

Learning involves more than being exposed to it.

There is a question in my mind as to whether we can have fully effective teachers if all of them go through college and then into teaching without more experience in the real world.

The social studies will more and more have to deal with the realities of how nations, peoples, and individuals live.

With respect to education, the drop in the birth rate is likely to be the most significant factor in years to come.

We have failed to see the effect upon the education needed by children of the shifting nature of our labor forces. This is one of the things we must cope with in the immediate future.

In the years ahead the teaching profession may find it difficult to realize that the schools cannot expect automatic increases in their expenditures.

In more general terms what I see ahead is the unceasing struggle of new nations to achieve some kind of stability. There will be continuing conflict among various groups trying to get control and sometimes other countries will be pulled into their troubles.

During the next 20 years there will rarely be a developing country that isn't in some kind of conflict as the effort to achieve political stability and economic development proceeds.

Guaranteed employment through the government is a possibility, but it can be a long-term reality only if it involves productive work that people value.

We must recognize the fact that we are not an affluent nation. We had been primarily a productive nation. Unless we can figure out how to keep increasing productivity, we cannot expect to have more and more to divide among us.

The so-called fundamental processes and ethical character are the two cardinal principles which have application throughout the arenas of life. Reading, for example, is a fundamental process that involves health, home membership, and all the rest.

The home has reduced its contributions to education in two ways: One is reflected in the increasing number of mothers who are now in the labor force. Many children don't have any home guidance. The second contribution the home has withdrawn is providing the kind of learning experiences that used to be a part of all children's backgrounds.

Part-time jobs and chores around home once gave children a chance to learn a good many things, as when they went to shop for mother. Today very few children compute the cost of what they buy at the grocery store.

The environment outside the school that used to provide education has been slipping away. The school should do whatever it can to develop supportive experiences outside the school walls.

If you look at the cardinal principles, you will find that they do not distinguish between education in general for effective citizenship in a democracy and what the *schools* can do about it.

Actually, the educational system has been, in a broad sense, a system composed of home, of work place, and religious institutions as well as the school. There has been rapid erosion of much of this system. Only the school has the same number of hours devoted to educational experiences that it had 25 years ago.

The cardinal principles, by overpromising, gave erroneous impressions of what the schools should do. The schools can't do everything; we have got to talk more sensibly about what the schools actually can do.

I foresee a time when the older people will organize politically to fight inflation and children and youth will demand attention because they will have so few adequate employment opportunities. It is my impression that things will achieve a balance sometime around 2000.

Wedgeworth, Robert, Jr.:

We are actually losing channels of communication when we most need them.

Agencies other than schools must share the enormous burden of educating the young and the old.

Wise, Helen D.:

We haven't realized that we aren't considered as a world leader by many countries because they simply aren't looking at the same goals we are.

I would suggest two major premises. One is that there should be increased emphasis on lifelong learning. The second imperative is that we have to have a great deal more flexibility for in-and-out of education.

I think the seven cardinal principles have great merit even now.

The fundamental processes involve learning how to learn.

APPENDIX B
COPING, CARING, COMMUNICATING,
YOUTH LOOKS AT THE FUTURE

by Catherine McKenzie Shane

Despite our sometimes harsh treatment and stern disciplining of the young in a traditional work ethic, Americans have historically prized and appreciated their young people. We virtually invented the concept of a happy childhood during the 1920s, probed the problems of youth in the Great Depression, created a permissive kingdom of the young in the 1950s, and listened to their ideas with a mixture of anxiety and delight during the 1960s. Gradually, oldsters came to envy the orange-juice-and-vitamin-fueled energy of youth and learned to listen with resignation to TV commercials aimed at children whose allowances and earnings in recent decades have literally run into the billions.

In this Bicentennial issue of the *Kappan,* it seems fitting to reflect our interest in the young—who are also our hope for the twenty-first century—by exploring their views on the design of the world they will begin increasingly to inherit between 1976 and 2001.

To gather material on how youth views the future, 95 junior and senior high students were interviewed last year in the United States and Great Britain. While respondents were not selected as national polling organizations choose a representative sample, the students were drawn from socioeconomic and ethnic groupings ranging from big-city private schools to rural public schools.* All the young

From the September 1976 issue of *Phi Delta Kappan.* Reprinted by permission of the publisher.

*The author acknowledges with appreciation the cooperation of the Calhoun School in New York City; the Strathclyde Educational Authority of Glasgow, Scotland; the Chicago and Houston public schools; and the Brown County (Indiana) public schools. Thanks also are due to the National Association of Secondary School Principals, which arranged to tape the views of state student council presidents during their annual meeting, held under NASSP auspices in Washington, D.C.

people who were taped were articulate, thoughtful, and willing to discuss freely their views of the future and the current and future role of schools. The group interviews were conducted in an informal manner with no school personnel present. Prior to each interview, the students were given an outline of the general topics which would be covered. They were asked not to bring notes with them and were encouraged to be open and candid throughout the discussion.

During the interviews, students were asked to respond to the following questions:

1. What will the world be like in the year 2000? Are you optimistic or pessimistic about the future? What are some of your hopes and fears about the future?
2. What can schools and teachers do now to help students better prepare for the year 2000?
3. Of the seven cardinal principles of education,* which do you consider to be the most important?

YOUTH LOOKS AT THE FUTURE.   Discussing some of the global problems they will confront over the next quarter century, the youngsters were cautiously optimistic, although many of them saw "drastic changes" occurring within their lifetime. They envisioned an increasingly complex and stressful world, one which would call for greater flexibility and ability to cope with difficult problems. In some ways, the youngsters saw themselves as a "lost generation," seeking meaning and direction in a bewildering world of change and challenge.

The following quotations, taken from the eight interviews conducted, summarize the youngsters' thinking about the future in general. (Respondents were white unless otherwise noted.)

> Things are going to be drastically different. We're going to have to cope with a pressing energy crisis and learn to eat different kinds of foods. Transportation and housing will have to change, too, because of the population growth.   —Houston junior (black)

---

*As identified in 1918 by a National Education Association commission, education's seven goals were health, command of fundamental processes, worthy home membership, vocation, citizenship, worthy use of leisure, and ethical character.

If there's room left in the world by the year 2000, there's going to be a lot more stress than there is now.
—Southwest state student council president

I'm an optimist, but a cautious one. We have to have hope for the future, but we just can't go into things blindly optimistic.
—Mountain state student council president

In our lifetime, we won't see the world we'd like to see.
—Scottish senior high student.

I'm optimistic because a lot of young people today are starting to become concerned about issues and about how things are going to be in the world.
—Rural Indiana senior

Several specific areas of concern, summarized below, emerged during discussions of the future.

Materialism.   With few exceptions, the students were sharply critical of the importance their society places on material goods and possessions. Somewhat naively, many longed for a return to "the simple life of our forefathers," although the youngsters did not identify precisely what "the simple life" was—with the exception of one New York senior, a girl, who wanted to spend the rest of her life "away from it all" on a horse farm.

Happiness in America is the fourth car in the driveway and a color TV in each room.
—New York junior

The U.S. has only 5% of the world's population, but we consume 25% of the world's raw materials and 60% of its consumer goods. That's scary.
—Chicago junior (Mexican-American)

Like, the United States is on this capitalistic kick. Just get money and things. Just get up as high as you can go.
—Chicago senior (Latino)

We have to reevaluate our values. People are beginning to realize that they have overindulged in things. We have to look at life's basics and sort out what things are important.
—Mountain state student council president

Technology.   A large number of youngsters expressed concern that technology in its many forms would lead to a complex, machine-dominated society, a society which might ultimately lead to their destruction or one in which they could possibly lose their individuality. Throughout the discussions, "technology" was frequently associated with "problems," "materialism," and "loss of identity."

> We're headed toward a technological crisis where we have two options: First, we destory ourselves trying to look for more technological advances or, second, we get away from technological materialism and back into a basic system of life like our forefathers had.
>
> —West Coast state student council president

> We won't be around in the year 2000. Our technology will lead to a nuclear holocaust that will destroy us all.
>
> —East Coast state student council president

> With technology, it seems like it brings about more problems that offset the proportion of our advances.   —Chicago senior (black)

World Citizenship.   With one exception—a rural Indiana youngster who felt that "the U.S. is going to have to concentrate a lot more on itself without worrying about every little country that has problems"—the students agreed that "worthy world membership" was essential for the future survival of humankind.

The question of "have" and "have-not" nations was frequently raised, with the U.S. being identified as an over-consuming "have" nation. American youngsters were especially concerned about the fate of nations less affluent than their own, while the British students tended to be more insular in their thinking—possibly because of the economic problems currently facing inflation-torn Britain.

The theme of interdependence among different races and cultures ran strongly throughout the dialogues with all groups interviewed, the black students being particularly eloquent in voicing their hopes for greater interracial understanding.

> We're going to have to depend a lot more on each other if we're going to survive. We should learn more about other races and cultures so we can understand them better.
>
> —Houston senior (Mexican-American)

> It's very essential that we try to get more and more cooperation between the nations. We're all together in one world. We need to

help one another. Like, you can't have the people of India starving
while we've got plenty of food here.   —Chicago junior (black)

I'd add worthy world membership as the eighth cardinal principle.
—Scottish senior

We need a more social education to help us take a more balanced
look at others and remove ignorance and barriers between nations.
—Chicago senior (black)

Government.   In each of the eight interviews, the students
identified government—both at the national and international
levels—as one of their main concerns. Post-Watergate disillusionment may have caused many of the young people to be sharply
critical of government. Few youngsters believed the government
works effectively for the people. Many wanted to see changes in
government at all levels, yet hesitated to cite specific areas for
improvement.

A surprising number of students stated that a totalitarian, Communist form of government would, quite possibly, take over the
entire Western world by the third millenium. Asked why this might
be so, students identified breakdowns in authority within the
government, with various factions working at cross purposes,
frequently for selfish interests.

Looking at future trends within world government, some
students saw an authoritarian/totalitarian form of government as
being necessary for the survival of humankind. However, none of
the young people interviewed had any comment to make about life
in countries currently under Communist control.

How can we improve our government? They just tell us to vote.
But that's only part of the answer.   —New York senior

I'm pessimistic about the government because you have so many
men working against each other. They're out for themselves, and not
the people.   —Chicago senior (Mexican-American)

The government? It can't get any worse. When you're at the bot-
ton, you've got nowhere to go but up. On the news the other day, I
heard that a committee is going to try and get the government back
in touch with the people.   —Rural Indiana junior

Government is going to have to become more authoritarian and
totalitarian if we're going to survive worldwide food shortages and
the population explosion.   —Houston senior

We need to form a world government—a sort of global imperialism in which we're all pulling together.   —Scottish senior

The politicians are out of touch with the people. Communism will take over.   —Rural Indiana senior

Schools have to teach people how to change—give us an open mind so that we can cope with change when it comes.   —New York senior

As the world becomes more complex, there's a loss of individual identity. And that's what schools must combat in the future—be more conscious of us as individuals.   —Houston senior

School's a great place to be. Like, it's like your house. The teachers make you feel at home. They crack jokes with you, but you still get your work done.

—Drop-in student, Chicago industrial arts center

YOUTH LOOK AT SCHOOLS AND TEACHERS.   It should come as no surprise to learn that the young people interviewed had their "finest hour" talking about schools and teachers. To their credit, the youngsters avoided the temptation of taking pot-shots at those who were not present. They were, on the whole, appreciative of the job that schools are doing despite drawbacks—lack of money and large class size were cited most often.

Implicit within the quotes that follow are three areas of concern which each group of young people persistently brought up during the interviews:

1. The need for schools to help young people *cope* with an increasingly changing and complex world
2. The need for schools to show that they *care* about young people as individuals
3. The need for homes and schools to *communicate* more effectively with youngsters, many of whom feel that they are in a communications vacuum in which their peers are the sole communicators

Schools should teach us about the realities of life and how to cope with problems that will come up in the future.

—West Coast state student council president

Schools should make us more aware of ourselves and of the world outside the school walls.   —Scottish senior

All things considered, like lack of money and big classes, I think schools do a good job. I mean, you can't always do what you want to do. Somebody always had to get you to move your butt.
—Rural Indiana senior

School is just busy-work. You do the same things over and over and over again. But there are so many kids at so many different levels. So how come we're all learning the same things at the same pace? —Rural Indiana junior

Schools should teach us all the different alternatives that are open to society, but they should also show that there's a basic foundation to life. —Northeast state student council president

Schools should give us guidance to understand the nature of life and existence. I find myself in a vacuum groping for the meaning of life. —Scottish senior girl

Testing. During the discussions on schools and schooling, each group of youngsters made special mention of tests and testing. Many of the students complained about the futility of tests—of testing for testing's sake—of tests' failing to measure their real capabilities as students.

Frequently, testing was associated with lack of interest in the students as individuals and was regarded as a copout device: to avoid working with students on a one-to-one basis.

The need for individualized instruction, with each student progressing at his own rate, was invariably mentioned by the young people as a viable alternative to testing.

I think tests are a gyp. You're pressured into them and if you mess up on them you're made to think you won't make it anywhere. I don't think that's education. I think that's just scaring a kid half to death. —Rural Indiana youngster

When we're tested, we're not tested on our knowledge or what we really know. It's just what they [the teachers] *think* we should know.
—Houston senior (black)

Tests don't show what quality you have as a person.
—Houston senior (Mexican-American)

About Teachers. Are there any good teachers left in this world? According to the youths interviewed, yes, there are! Asked to describe the "good" teacher, youngsters responded as follows:

> I saw a cartoon the other day where two small kids went up to their mom and said: "Mom! Mom! We just saw Miss Higgins, our teacher, and she was hugging and kissing a man." And they looked at their mom and said: "Can teachers be people, too?"
>
> —New York senior

> Good teachers show us that they're people, too.
>
> —West Coast state student council president

> The best teacher I ever had . . . she didn't give you busy-work, like read then answer questions. She let you speak and listened to your opinions. She helped us think about ourselves. In her classroom, the class was run by the class.   —Chicago junior (black)

> Good teachers let you talk and they listen.
>
> —Chicago senior (black)

> We've got great teachers. They're like family. They respect us and joke with us and we work together.
>
> —Drop-in student, Chicago industrial arts center

> In a lot of countries, like Russia, the teachers are like second parents. When I was in second grade, that's the way it was. My mom, she'd say to me: "O.K. The teacher's going to be your mother now for eight hours. *You listen to her!*" We need more of that.
>
> —Houston Chinese-American

> We're very close to the teachers in my school. They treat us with respect, like we're on the same level.   —New York senior

Two general areas of teacher criticism emerged during the conversations with students.

1. Youngsters complained that teachers do not have, or do not want, to take the time to communicate with individual students. The majority of students interviewed wanted to have more discussion time with their teachers, in order to have a freer exchange of ideas. (It is interesting to note that at the end of every interview, at least three of four students stayed behind to thank the interviewer for taking the time to talk to them and listen to their opinions.)
2. Teachers are failing to help students prepare for the world of today and tomorrow because they reflect the world of yesterday, teaching what they were taught. Many youngsters felt that teachers were not keeping up with emerging trends and ideas.

The following excerpts from dialogues with youth are representative of the youngsters' thinking:

> Computers will not take the place of the teacher. Everybody needs somebody to talk to and you couldn't really go up to a computer and ask it for help. We need to talk with teachers more.
>
> —Houston junior (black)

> The teachers are teaching what they were taught. But things have changed and we don't live in their world. They [the teachers] haven't kept up with what's going on. But they're caught in the middle. They have to do what the administration tells them to do.
>
> —Rural Indiana senior

> Like we've got this English teacher. All he can talk about is stuff he learned in college. I don't want to know about that. Why can't we get with some of the good books on today's scene?   —Chicago senior

ASSESSMENT OF THE CARDINAL PRINCIPLES. During the pilot interviews for the project, I asked participating students to comment on the relevance of each of the seven cardinal principles of education as they were originally outlined by the National Education Association's Commission on the Reorganization of Secondary Education in 1918. It became apparent after a couple of interviews that the youngsters were interested in discussing only those principles which they considered to be of prime importance—even although they regarded all seven as still being valid today (some being more valid than others).

Health and worthy use of leisure time were not regarded by students as the responsibility of schools, but of the home or social agencies outside the school. Some students felt that the development of ethical character is the responsibility of the church and home rather than the school. In contrast, others wanted the school to assume more responsibility for the moral and ethical development of students, since the church and home appear to be failing to give adequate direction.

The disillusionment which the young people felt about government at all levels tended to cloud their thinking about the importance of civic education in the school curriculum. A "what's the good of knowing about civics if government doesn't work" cynicism dominated many of the discussions.

Three of the seven cardinal principles were identified by all groups of students as being the most important. In order, these were:

1. *Command of fundamental processes.* The three Rs were considered to be of primary importance in the learning process. Many students wanted to see elementary schools do a better job in teaching the fundamentals, thus giving youngsters greater freedom of choice in selecting subjects which interest them when they reach high school.

2. *Vocational competence.* It was interesting to note during the discussions about vocational competence the unconscious distinction made by many youngsters about "the school world" and "the real world" or "work world." With few exceptions, the students felt that school should provide greater work/learning experiences outside of school walls. Greater flexibility of time, inside and outside of school hours, together with increased curriculum offerings in the vocational skills, were felt to be essential if schools are to prepare their students to enter "the real world."

During rap sessions at the end of the interviews, students were asked what they planned to do following graduation. Most of the American youngsters planned to go to college and into some type of service work. Conservation, psychology, nursing, teaching, and social work were only a few of the service-oriented jobs mentioned. None of the American students thought of education as a means "to make money." This was in distinct contrast with their British counterparts, many of whom planned to go to the university, "get a degree, and then get a good job to make money." Among the career choices of the British youngsters interviewed were the "established" professions of law, engineering, medicine, and economics.

Worthy home membership. Of all the seven cardinal principles discussed, students were most willing to talk about the role of the family in their lives. The quotations which follow disquietingly reveal the isolation which many young people feel today. While it was encouraging to hear some youngsters speak of their families with love and affection, it was also saddening to hear equally as many talk of their feelings of distance from their family. The following quotations reflect the most frequently voiced concerns of the young people interviewed:

> When I was a little kid, when I had trouble spelling a word, my mother would sit down with me and we'd go over the stuff together. Now today, the mothers because of their work, they don't have time to help the kids. They figure that's what teachers get paid for—so let *them* teach the kids. So the kids come home and they're having problems and the mothers say: "Oh, go play outside and get off my back."
>
> —Chicago senior

> It used to be that families had to stay close together, like in the Depression, in order to survive. Now, there's much more stress on individuality. Like, I'm a female and it used to be that my role would be to marry and raise a family. I don't look at it that way. What if I want to follow a career? There goes the family bit.
>
> —Rural Indiana junior

> You used to have a grandmother live at your house and your parents and maybe some other relatives. Now everybody's scattered. There's not all that much family around that you can talk to. So we talk to other kids. I don't hardly see my folks until the weekend. Dad works nights and Mom during the day. The only time I get to see them is at weekends . . . when we're together we don't talk about things, we just sit and watch TV.
>
> —Rural Indiana senior

> I just tried to tell my mom how I felt and she got real mad. I just wanted her to know how I feel.
>
> —Houston junior (Mexican-American)

IN RETROSPECT. It was an impressive and at times moving experience to work with young people on this project. Without exception, the youngsters came across as thoughtful, articulate, and insightful people who cared about their world and showed considerable knowledge of the problems confronting us on a national and global scale. It struck me as being somewhat ironic that, despite the students' gripes about schools and schooling, they should come through so well in the interviews. Obviously, someone somewhere is doing a good job!

CATHERINE McKENZIE SHANE, a Scot by birth, studied at Jordanhill College of Education in Glasgow, Scotland, to become an elementary school teacher. She also studied voice and piano at the Royal Scottish Academy of Music and holds graduate degrees, magna cum laude, in English and philosophy from DePaul University and Northwestern University in Chicago.

Mrs. Shane is the author of a number of books and filmstrips for young people. A major work is the 16-volume set of Compton's Precyclopedia *for young children. Formerly senior editorial vice-president for* Compton's Encyclopedia, *a division of* Encyclopaedia Britannica, *Mrs. Shane now lives in Bloomington, Indiana, where she likes "to play with children, play the piano, and play golf."*

SELECTED READINGS

Many of the recent books dealing with world trends, problems of the present, and probable alternative futures are not widely read by teachers. The following bibliography may prove of interest to teachers who seek additional information.

Anderson, Robert H., Millie Almy, Harold G. Shane, and Ralph Tyler. *Education in Anticipation of Tomorrow.* Worthington, Ohio: Charles A. Jones, 1973.

Ayres, Robert V. *Technological Forecasting and Long-Range Planning.* New York: Holt, Rinehart and Winston, 1971.

Baier, Kurt, and Nicholas Rescher, eds. *Values and the Future.* New York: Free Press, 1969.

Beckwith, Burnham P. *The Next 500 Years.* New York: Beckwith Press, 1967.

Berkson, I. B. *Ethics, Politics, and Education.* Eugene: University of Oregon Books, 1968.

Bhagwati, Jagdish N. *Economics and World Order: From the 1970's to the 1990's.* New York: Macmillan, 1973.

Black, C. E. *The Dynamics of Modernization.* New York: Harper & Row, 1966.

Boguslaw, Robert. *The New Utopians.* Englewood Cliffs, N. J.: Prentice-Hall, 1965.

Bookchin, Murray. *The Limits of the City.* New York: Harper and Row, 1974.

Bright, James R. *A Brief Introduction to Technology Forecasting: Concepts and Exercises.* New York: Permaquid Press, 1972.

_____, ed. *Technological Forecasting for Industry and Government: Methods and Applications.* Englewood Cliffs, N. J.: Prentice-Hall, 1968.

Brown, Lester R., *In the Human Interest.* New York: W. W. Dutton, 1974.

_____. *Twenty-two Dimensions of the Population Problem,* Worldwatch Paper #5. Washington, D.C.: Worldwatch Institute, 1976.

_____. *World without Borders.* New York: Random House, 1972.

Bundy, Robert, ed. *Images of the Future: The Twenty-first Century and Beyond.* Buffalo, N. Y.: Prometheus Books, 1976.

Calder, Nigel. *Technopolis, the Social Control of the Uses of Science.* Norwich, England: Fletcher and Son (Panther Books Edition), 1970.

Case, Charles W., and Paul A. Olson. *The Future: Create or Inherit.* Lincoln: University of Nebraska Press, 1974.

Cellarius, Richard A., and John Platt. "Councils of Urgent Studies." *Science* 177:670–676; August 25, 1972.

Charter, S. P. R. *The Choice and the Threat.* New York: Ballentine Books, 1972.

Chase, Stuart. *The Most Probable World.* New York: Harper and Row, 1968.

Clark, Richard E. "Recent Trends in Computer Assisted Instruction," An ERIC Paper issued by the ERIC Clearinghouse On Media and Technology. Stanford, Calif.: Stanford University Press, 1973.

Clarke, Arthur C. *Profiles of the Future.* New York: Bantam Books, 1963.

Cole, H. S. D., Christopher Freeman, Marie Jahoda, and K. L. R. Pavitt, eds. *Models of Doom: A Critique of the Limits to Growth.* New York: Universe Books, 1973.

Commoner, Barry. *The Closing Circle.* New York: Alfred A. Knopf, 1971.

Cox, Harvey. *The Seduction of the Spirit.* New York: Simon and Schuster, 1973.

Dale, Edgar. *Building a Learning Environment.* Bloomington, Ind.: Phi Delta Kappa Foundation, 1972.

Dalkey, Norman C., and Daniel L. Rourke. *Experimental Assessment of Delphi Procedures with Group Value Judgments.* Santa Monica, Calif.: RAND Corp., 1971.

de Brigard, Raul, and Olaf Helmer. *Some Potential Developments, 1970–2000.* Middletown, Conn.: Institute for the Future, 1970.

de Chardin, Teilhard. *The Future of Man.* London: William Collins Sons, 1959.

———. *The Phenomenon of Man.* New York: Harper and Row, 1955.

de Jouvenel, Bertrand. *The Art of Conjecture.* New York: Basic Books, 1967.

de Ropp, Robert S. *The New Prometheans.* New York: Delta Books, 1972.

De Voto, Bernard. "The Century." *Harper's Magazine* 201:49–58; October 1950.

Dickson, Paul. *Think Tanks.* New York: Atheneum, 1971.

Dobzhansky, Theodosius. *The Biology of Ultimate Concern.* London: Collins Press, 1971.

Drucker, Peter F. *The Age of Discontinuity.* New York: Harper and Row, 1969.

———. *Management.* New York: Harper and Row, 1974.

———. "Saving the Crusade." *Harper's Magazine* 244:66–71; January 1972.

Eckholm, Erik. *Losing Ground.* New York: W. W. Norton, 1976.

Elliott, Katherine, ed. *The Family and Its Future.* Ciba Foundation Blueprint. London: J. & A. Churchill, 1970.

Ellul, Jacques. *The Technological Society.* New York: Vintage Books, 1967.

Ewald, William R., Jr. *Environment and Change.* Bloomington: Indiana University Press, 1968.

_____. *Environment and Policy.* Bloomington: Indiana University Press, 1968.

"The Exploration of the Future," *Réalités* 245:50–58; June 1966. (Translated from the French by R. Neiswender for the RAND collection, p. 3540, February 1957).

"Faut-il Stopper La Société de Consommation?" *Paris Match* July 1972, pp. 40–57.

Feinberg, Gerald. *The Prometheus Project.* New York: Doubleday, 1969.

Fergeson, Marilyn. *The Brain Revolution.* New York: Taplinger, 1973.

Forrester, Jay W. *Urban Dynamics.* Cambridge, Mass.: M.I.T. Press, 1969.

_____. *World Dynamics.* Cambridge, Mass.: Wright-Allen Press, 1971.

Friere, Paulo. *Education for Critical Consciousness.* New York: Seabury Press, 1973.

_____. *Pedagogy of the Oppressed.* New York: Herder and Herder, 1972.

Fuller, Buckminster. "Geoview: Heartbeats and Illions." *World* 2:44–45; March 13, 1973.

_____. "Thinking Out Loud: Disproving the Population Explosion," *World* July 13, 1973, pp. 16–40. (Part I of a three-part series.)

Gabor, Dennis. *The Mature Society.* New York: Praeger, 1972.

Galbraith, John Kenneth. *The New Industrial State.* Boston: Houghton Mifflin, 1967.

Gannon, Colin A. *An Introduction to the Study of Technological Change and Its Consequences for Regional and Community Development.* Springfield, Ill.: Department of Business and Economic Development, 1967.

Gardner, John W. *The Recovery of Confidence.* New York: Pocket Books, 1971.

_____. *Self-Renewal.* New York: Harper and Row, 1964.

George, Robley E. *Common Sense II.* New York: Exposition Press, 1972.

Glass, Bentley. "Evolution in Human Hands." *Phi Delta Kappan* 50:506–510; May 1969.

_____. *The Timely and the Timeless: The Interrelationships of Science, Education and Society.* New York: Basic Books, 1970.

Goodlad, John I. *Schooling for the Future.* Los Angeles: Educational Inquiry, 1971.

Gordon, Kermit. *Agenda for the Nation.* Garden City, N.Y.: Doubleday, 1968.

Gordon, Theodore J. *Forecasts of Some Technological and Scientific Developments and Their Societal Consequences.* Middletown, Conn.: Institute for the Future, 1969.

————. *The Future.* New York: St. Martin's Press, 1965.

Gray, Elizabeth, D. D. Gray, and William F. Martin. *Growth and Its Implications for the Future.* Branford, Conn.: The Dinosaur Press, 1975.

Green, Thomas, ed. *Educational Planning in Perspective.* Guildford, Surrey, England: IPC Science and Technology Press, 1971.

Halacy, D. S., Jr. *Your City Tomorrow.* New York: Four Winds Press, 1973.

"The Half Century," *Time* 55:26–43; January 2, 1950.

Hall, Edward T. *Beyond Culture.* Garden City, N.Y.: Anchor Press/Doubleday, 1976.

————. *The Hidden Dimension.* Garden City, N.Y.: Doubleday, 1966.

————. *The Silent Language.* Garden City, N.Y.: Doubleday, 1959.

Handler, Philip. *Biology and the Future of Man.* New York: Oxford University Press, 1970.

Hardin, Garrett. "The Tragedy of the Commons." *Science,* December 13, 1968, pp. 1243–1248.

Harman, Willis W. *Alternative Futures and Educational Policy.* Menlo Park, Calif.: Stanford Research Institute, 1970.

Harrington, Michael. *The Accidental Century.* Baltimore, Md.: Penguin Books, 1965.

Heilbroner, Robert. *Inquiry into the Human Prospect.* New York: W. W. Norton, 1974.

————. "Second Thoughts on *The Human Prospect,*" *Futures,* February 1976, pp. 31–40.

Helmer, Olaf. *Social Technology.* New York: Basic Books, 1966.

Hirsch, Werner Z., ed. *Inventing Education for the Future.* San Francisco: Chandler, 1967.

Hostrop, Richard W., ed. *Foundations of Futurology in Education.* Homewood, Ill.: ETC Publications, 1973.

Hudson Institute Study. *The Corporate Environment, 1975–1985.* Croton-on-Hudson, N.Y.: Hudson Institute, 1971.

"Huxley Sees 1980's as a Perilous Time." *New York Times,* October 12, 1969.

Illich, Ivan. *Tools for Conviviality.* New York: Harper and Row, 1973.

Jencks, Christoper. *Inequality: A Reassessment of the Effect of Family and Schooling in America.* New York: Basic Books, 1972.

Kahn, Herman. "The Squaring of America." *Intellectual Digest* 3:16–19; September 1972.

————, and Bruce B. Briggs. *Things To Come: Thinking about the 70's and 80's.* New York: Macmillan, 1972.

————, and Anthony J. Wiener. *The Year 2000: A Framework for Speculation.* New York: Macmillan, 1967.

Kauffman, Draper L., Jr. *Teaching the Future.* Palm Springs, Calif.: ETC Publications, 1976.

Kilpatrick, William H. *Education for a Changing Society.* New York: Macmillan, 1926.

Kostelanetz, Richard. *Social Speculations: Visions for Our Time.* New York: William Morrow, 1971.

Krech, David. "Psychoneurobiochemeducation." *Phi Delta Kappan* 50:370–375; March 1969.

"Les Savants Scrutent l'Avenir." *Réalitiés* 237:106–111; Octobre 1965.

Little, Dennis L., and Theodore J. Gordon. *Some Trends Likely To Affect American Society in the Next Several Decades.* Middletown, Conn.: Institute for the Future, 1971.

Longstreet, Wilma. *Beyond Jencks: The Myth of Equal Schooling.* Washington, D.C.: Association for Supervision and Curriculum Development, 1973.

McHale, John. *The Future of the Future.* New York: George Braziller, 1969.

McLuhan, Marshall, and Edmund Carpenter, eds. *Explorations in Communications.* Boston: Beacon Press, 1960.

———, and George B. Leonard. "The Future of Education: The Class of 1989." *Look* February 21, 1967.

Madden, Carl H. *Clash of Culture: Management in an Age of Changing Values.* Washington, D.C.: National Planning Association, 1972.

Maddox, John. *The Doomsday Syndrome.* New York: McGraw-Hill, 1972.

Marien, Michael. *Alternative Futures for Learning, an Annotated Bibliography.* Syracuse, N.Y.: Educational Policy Research Center, 1971.

———. *Essential Reading for the Future of Education,* Rev. Syracuse, N.Y.: Educational Policy Research Center, 1971. Annotated supplement to the original Marien bibliography, *Alternative Futures for Learning.*

———, ed. *The Hot List Delphi: An Exploratory Survey of Essential Reading for the Future.* Syracuse, N.Y.: University Research Corp., 1972.

———, and Warren Z. Ziegler, eds. *The Potential of Educational Futures,* The NSSE Series, "Contemporary Educational Issues." Worthington, Ohio: Charles A. Jones, 1972.

Meachen, Robert Neil. *Technological Forecasting, a Bibliography.* Coventry, England: Codig Liaison Centre, 1971.

Meadows, D. H., *et al. The Limits to Growth.* London: Earth Island, 1972.

Medawar, Sir Peter. *The Hope of Progress.* London: Methuen, 1972.

Meeker, Robert J., and Daniel M. Weiler. *A New School for the Cities.* Santa Monica, Calif.: System Development Corp., 1970.

Michael, Donald N. "L'Avenie du Temps Libre." *Economie et Humanisme* 167:3–12; Mai/Juin 1966.

———. *The Next Generation.* New York: Random House, 1963.

———. *The Unprepared Society: Planning for a Precarious Future.* New York: Basic Books, 1968.

Midwest Public Relations Conference, University of Wisconsin, 1965.

Coping with Change. Report Compiled by Journalism Extension Services, Madison, 1966.

Miller, Delbert C. *Leadership and Power in the Bos-Wash Megalopolis.* New York: John Wiley, 1975.

Moon, Rexford G., Jr. *National Planning for Education.* New York: Academy for Educational Development, 1970.

Morphet, Edgar, and David L. Jesser, eds. *Cooperative Planning for Education in 1980, Designing Education for the Future.* No. 4. New York: Citation Press, 1968.

————, and David L. Jesser, eds. *Emerging Designs for Education, Designing Education for the Future,* No. 5. New York: Citation Press, 1968.

————, and David J. Jesser, eds. *Planning for Effective Utilization of Technology in Education: Designing Education for the Future,* No. 6. New York: Citation Press, 1969.

————, and Charles O. Ryan, eds. *Implications for Education of Prospective Changes in Society, Designing Education for the Future,* No. 2. New York: Citation Press, 1967.

————, and Charles O. Ryan, eds. *Planning and Effecting Needed Changes in Education, Designing Education for the Future,* No. 3. New York: Citation Press, 1967.

————, and Charles O. Ryan, eds. *Prospective Changes in Society by 1980, Designing Education for the Future,* No. 1. New York: Citation Press, 1967.

Morrison, Elting Elmore. *Men, Machines, and Modern Times.* Cambridge, Mass.: M.I.T. Press, 1966.

Muller, Herbert J. *Children of Frankenstein: A Primer on Modern Technology and Human Values.* Bloomington: Indiana University Press, 1971.

Mumford, Lewis. *The Pentagon of Power.* New York: Harcourt Brace Jovanovich, 1964.

Nelson, Richard R., *et al. Technology, Economic Growth, and Public Policy.* A RAND Corp. and Brookings Institute Study. Washington, D.C., 1967.

Nobile, Philip, ed. *The Con III Controversy.* New York: Pocket Books, 1971.

Nordhaus, William D. *Invention, Growth, and Welfare: A Theoretical Treatment of Technological Change.* Cambridge, Mass.: M.I.T. Press, 1969.

Olson, Paul A., Larry Freeman, and James Bowman, eds. *Education for 1984 and After.* Lincoln, Nebr.: Study Commission on Undergraduate Education and the Education of Teachers, 1971.

Patterson, Wade N. Review of *Education in Anticipation of Tomorrow,* edited by Robert H. Anderson. November 1973.

Perisco, Connell F., and Norman B. McEachron. *Forces for Societal Transportation in the United States, 1950–2000.* Menlo Park, Calif.: Stanford Research Institute, 1971.

Perloff, Harvey S., ed. *The Future of the U.S. Government.* Englewood Cliffs, N.J.: Prentice-Hall, 1971.

Pines, Maya. *The Brain Changers.* New York: Harcourt Brace Jovanovich, 1973.

Platt, John. "A Fearful and Wonderful World for Living." Paper presented at the Home Economics Centennial Symposium, Families of the Future. Ames, Iowa, October 5, 1971. (Mimeo.)

_____. "How Men Can Shape Their Futures." *Futures* 3:32–47; March 1971.

_____. "Science for Human Survival." *The Science Teacher* 40:1; January 1973.

_____. "What We Must Do." *Science* 166:1115–1121; November 28, 1969.

Postman, Neil. "The New Literacy." *Grade Teacher* March 1971.

Reich, Charles A. *The Greening of America.* New York: Bantam, 1971.

Revel, Jean-François. *Without Marx or Jesus.* Garden City, N.Y.: Doubleday, 1971.

Rogers, Everett M. *Communication of Innovations, a Cross-Cultural Approach.* New York: Free Press, 1971.

Rosenfeld, Stephen S. "Robert S. McNamara and the Wiser Use of Power." *World,* July 13, 1973, pp. 18–24.

Roszak, Theodore. *The Making of a Counter Culture.* Garden City, N.Y.: Doubleday, 1969.

_____. *Where the Wasteland Ends.* Garden City, N.Y.: Doubleday, 1972.

Rubin, Louis, ed. *The Future of Education: Perspectives on Tomorrow's Schooling.* Boston: Allyn & Bacon, 1975.

Salk, Jonas. *The Survival of the Wisest.* New York: Harper and Row, 1973.

Savage, John A. Review of *The Schools Next Time: Explorations in Educational Sociology,* by Donald R. Thomas. November 1973.

Saylor, Galen J. *The School of the Future Now.* Washington, D.C.: Association for Supervision and Curriculum Development, 1972.

Schumacher, E. F. *Small is Beautiful.* New York: Harper and Row, 1973.

Shane, Harold G. "America's Educational Futures; 1976–2001: The Views of 50 Distinguished World Citizens and Educators." *The Futurists* 10:252–257; October 1976.

_____. "America's Next 25 Years: Some Implications for Education." *Phi Delta Kappan* 58:78–83; September 1976.

_____. "The Seven Cardinal Principles of Education Revisited." *Today's Education* 65:57–72; September–October 1976.

_____. "The Educational Significance of the Future." Mimeographed. A special report to the U.S. Commissioner of Education, 1972.

_____. *The Educational Significance of the Future.* Bloomington, Ind.: Phi Delta Kappa, 1973.

————. "The Future as a Force on Curriculum Change." *Phi Delta Kappan* 57:13–15; September 1975.

————. "Future-Planning as a Means of Shaping Educational Change," Chapter VIII in *The Curriculum: Retrospect and Prospect.* The 70th Yearbook of the NSSE, Part I. Chicago: University of Chicago Press, 1971.

————. "Future Shock and the Curriculum." *Phi Delta Kappan* 49:67–70; October 1967.

————. "Looking to the Future: Reassessment of Educational Issues of the 1970's." *Phi Delta Kappan* 54:326–337; January 1973.

————. "Making Tomorrow Work in Education." *Educational Horizons* 54:111–118; Spring 1976.

————. "The Moral Choices Before Us." *Phi Delta Kappan* 56:707–711; June 1975.

————. "Prospects and Prerequisites for the Improvement of Elementary Education," Chapter XV in *The Elementary School in the United States.* The 72nd Yearbook of the NSSE, Part II. Chicago: University of Chicago Press, 1973.

————. "The Rediscovery of Purpose in Education." *Educational Leadership* 28:581–584; March 1971.

————. "Social Decisions and Educational Policy," in L. Rubin, ed., *The Future of Education.* Boston: Allyn & Bacon, 1975.

————. Review of *Educational Futurism, 1985* by Walter G. Hack. *Phi Delta Kappan,* December 1971, p. 253.

————, and Virgil Clift. "The Future, Social Decision, and Educational Change in Secondary Schools," in William VanTil, ed., *Issues in Secondary Education.* The 75th Yearbook of the NSSE. Chicago: University of Chicago Press, 1976.

————, and Owen Nelson. "What Will the Schools Become?" *Phi Delta Kappan,* 52:596–598; June 1971.

————, *et al.* Emerging Moral Dimensions in Society: Implications for Schooling.* Washington, D.C.: Association for Supervision and Curriculum Development, 1975.

————, *et al.* in H. Waddington, ed., *The Future as an Academic Discipline.* London: The Ciba Foundation, 1975.

Simmons, Daniel J. "Beware! The Three Rs Cometh." *Phi Delta Kappan* 55:492–495; March 1973.

Sine, Tom. "The Megamachine and the Schoolhouse." *Phi Delta Kappan* 55:470–473; March 1974.

Skinner, B. F. *Beyond Freedom and Dignity.* New York: Alfred A. Knopf, 1971.

"Slowdown on Research." *Time,* July 2, 1973, p. 46.

Soleri, Paolo. *Matter Becoming Spirit.* Garden City, N.Y.: Anchor Press/Doubleday, 1973.

"Split Views on America." *Time,* December 25, 1972 (European edition), p. 20.

Starr, Richard F. *The Beginning of the Future.* New York: McGraw-Hill, 1973.

Suppes, Patrick. "The Computer and Excellence." *Saturday Review,* January 14, 1967.

———. "Computer Technology and the Future of Education." *Phi Delta Kappan,* April 1968.

———. "The Uses of Computers in Education." *Scientific American* 215:206–208; July 23, 1966.

Taylor, Gordon R. *The Biological Time Bomb.* New York: World, 1968.

———. *The Doomsday Book: Can the World Survive?* New York: World, 1972.

Technological Forecasting and Social Change. Vols. 1 and 2; T, 174, A2, T 25. Indiana University Library, Bloomington, 1969–70 and 1970–71.

Terry, Mark. *Teaching for Survival.* New York: Ballantine Books, 1971.

Theobald, Robert. *Futures Conditional.* Indianapolis: Bobbs-Merrill, 1971.

Thompson, William I. *At the Edge of History.* New York: Harper & Row, 1971.

———. *Passages about Earth.* New York: Harper & Row, 1973.

Toffler, Alvin. *The Ecospasm Report.* New York: Bantam Books, 1975.

———. "The Future as a Way of Life." *Horizons,* Summer 1965.

———. *Future Shock.* New York: Random House, 1970.

———, ed. *Learning for Tomorrow.* New York: Random House, 1974.

"Toward a National Materials Policy." *World,* May 22, 1973.

Urban Institute. *The Struggle to Bring Technology to Cities.* Washington, D.C., 1971.

Venn, Grant. *Man, Education, and Manpower.* Washington, D.C.: The American Association of School Administrators, 1970.

Vizinczey, Stephen. *The Rules of Chaos.* New York: McCall, 1969.

Wagar, W. Warren. *Building the City of Man.* New York: Grossman, 1971.

Wallia, C. S., ed. *Toward Century 21.* New York: Basic Books, 1970.

Walter, W. Grey. *The Living Brain.* New York: W. W. Norton, 1963.

Ward, Barbara. *Spaceship Earth.* New York: Columbia University Press, 1966.

———, and René Dubos. *Only One Earth: The Care and Maintenance of a Small Planet.* New York: W. W. Norton, 1972.

Ways, Max. "The Road to 1977." *Fortune,* January 1967.

Weizenbaum, Joseph. *Computer Power and Human Reason.* San Francisco: W. H. Freeman, 1976.

Wills, Gordon, *et al.,* eds. *Technological Forecasting and Corporate Strategy.* London: Lockwood, 1969.

Wilson, Elizabeth C. "The Knowledge Machine." *Teachers College Record* 70:109–119; November 1968.

ACKNOWLEDGMENTS

Many persons in many places contributed to the present National Education Association Project, designed to reframe the seven cardinal principles of education and to make recommendations for curriculum change in an interdependent, global human community.

First of all, appreciation must be expressed for the prescience and vision of members of the NEA Bicentennial Committee, who conceived not only the inquiry on which this publication is based but also many other creative ideas preserved in the NEA *Bicentennial Ideabook.* Helen D. Wise and James A. Harris shared the chair for the committee, which included seven additional members: David Almada, Thomas G. Bush, Charles Juancito, Betty Reardon, Thomas Santesteban, Edith Swanson, and Pauline Yamashita.

Much appreciation also is due the Project Pre-Planning Committee, which gave generously of its time. In addition to offering sound, practical advice, this group also selected the distinguished world citizens and teachers who were interviewed in order to determine their views regarding cardinal premises to guide U.S. education. The Pre-Planning Committee included the following persons:[1]

Geraldine Bagby
Vice President, The
   Danforth Foundation

Terrel Bell
U.S. Commissioner of
   Education

Louise Berman
University of Maryland

Luvern Cunningham
Executive Director, San
   Francisco Schools
Commission

John B. Davis, Jr.
President, Macalester
   College

[1]The affiliations of the committee members are given as of the time the group was convened.

William Ellena
Superintendent of
    Schools, Charlottes-
    ville, Virginia,
    Public Schools

L. D. Haskew
The University of
    Texas—Austin

Robert Lipscomb
Alabama Education
    Association

Wilma Longstreet
University of
    Michigan—Flint

Alvin D. Loving, Sr.
Scholar in Residence,
    U.S. Office of Educa-
    tion

Fr. John Meyer
Executive Secretary, Na-
    tional Catholic Educa-
    tion Association

Bert Mogin
U.S. Office of Education

Charles M. Plummer
Project Assistant, In-
    diana University

Wilson Riles
State Superintendent of
    Instruction, California
    State Department of
    Instruction

Harold G. Shane
University Professor of
    Education, Indiana
    University

B. Othanel Smith
University of Illinois
    (Emeritus); University
    of South Florida
    (Emeritus)

Theodore R. Sizer
Headmaster, Phillips
    Academy

Helen Wise
Pennsylvania teacher;
    former NEA
    president

More than 50 persons were invited and agreed to serve on the International Panel to reframe the seven cardinal principles and to develop educational guidelines that anticipated the 21st century. Crowded or conflicting schedules reduced the final roster to 46:[2]

Amara, Roy	President, Institute for the Future
Baisinger, Grace C.	Former President, Parent-Teachers Association
Benevidez, Patricia	Teacher, Tacoma, Washington
Blakeslee, Donald	High school teacher, Rawlins, Wyoming
Blanchard, François	International Secretary, Syndicat National des Enseignements de Sécond Degré (France)
Bloom, Benjamin	Professor of Education, University of Chicago

[2]Positions listed are those held by panel participants at the time of their involvement in the NEA inquiry.

Boulding, Elise	Sociologist, University of Colorado, Boulder
Bowser, Vivian	Elementary school teacher, Houston, Texas
Brewton, Agnes	Teacher, Iowa
Brown, Lester R.	Futurist; President, Worldwatch Institute; author, *World Without Borders*
Bundy, McGeorge	President, Ford Foundation
Castro, Raul H.	Governor of Arizona
Clementi, Nick	High school student, Racine, Wisconsin
Cohen, Wilbur J.	Dean, School of Education, University of Michigan
Conover, Hobart H.	Chief, Bureau of Business Education, New York State Department of Education; immediate past Chairman of Board of Future Business Leaders of America (Phi Beta Lambda)
Cousins, Norman	Editor, *Saturday Review/World*
Cremin, Lawrence A.	President, Teachers College, Columbia University
Dror, Yehezkel	Professor, Hebrew University of Jerusalem, Israel
Elm, Lloyd	Institute for the Development of Indian Law
Forbes, Jack	Assistant Professor, University of California, Davis
Foy, Joe H.	President, Texas Natural Gas Company, Houston
Harman, Willis W.	Director, Center for Studies of Social Policy, Stanford Research Institute
Havighurst, Robert J.	Professor Emeritus, University of Chicago
Hesburgh, Theodore M.	President, University of Notre Dame
Jarvis, Fred	General Secretary, National Union of Teachers of England and Wales
Johnson, John H.	Editor-Publisher, *Ebony*
Laidlaw, John, Jr.	Chairman of the Board, Robert Crown Center for Health and Drug Education
Lear, Norman	Television producer of such programs as "All in the Family," "The Jeffersons," "Maude"
Mackenzie, Malcolm	University of Glasgow
McMurrin, Sterling	Distinguished Professor and Dean, Graduate School, University of Utah

Mink, Patsy Takemoto	Congresswoman, Hawaii
Nieto, Consuelo	Assistant Professor, California State University at Long Beach
Passow, A. Harry	Director, Division of Educational Institutions and Programs, Teachers College, Columbia University
Perry, Sir Walter	The Open University (England)
Ray, Doris	Teacher, Alaska
Rockefeller, David	Chairman of the Board, Chase Manhattan Bank
Rumberger, Dale	President, Student National Education Association, Washington, D.C.
Salk, Jonas	Director, Salk Institute for Biological Studies
Shelley, Sally Swing	Chief, Educational Information Programs, UN
Sipilä, Helvi	Chairperson, International Women's Year, UN; Assistant to Kurt Waldheim
Smilansky, Moshe	University of Tel Aviv, Israel
Tanaka, Paul	President, Association of Classroom Teachers, Tacoma, Washington
Terkel, Louis (Studs)	Radio commentator, Chicago; author, *Working*
Thompson, John M.	Secretary-General, World Confederation of Organizations of the Teaching Profession
Tyler, Ralph W.	Founding Director, Center for Advanced Studies in the Behavioral Sciences, Stanford; Chairman, National Commission for Cooperative Education; Chairman, National Commission of Resources for Youth
Wedgeworth, Robert, Jr.	Executive Director, American Library Association
Wise, Helen D.	Pennsylvania teacher; Past President, NEA; Chairman, Bicentennial Committee

At the suggestion of the Pre-Planning Committee, a number of youth of secondary school age were interviewed in order to ascertain their thinking on questions analagous to those considered by the panel. Thanks are due the following people, who set up interviews with 95 juniors and seniors in their schools or districts:

Robert Calabrese	Administrative Assistant to the Superintendent, Brown County School Corporation, Nashville, Indiana
Eugene Ruth	Director, The Calhoun School, New York City
Lorraine Sullivan	Assistant Superintendent, Curriculum, The Chicago, Illinois Public Schools (two sets of interviews)
Daniel Burns	Deputy Director of Education, Glasgow, Scotland; Strathclyde Regional Council
Gonzalo Garza	Deputy Superintendent, General Instructional Services, The Houston, Texas, Independent School District

Thanks also are due the National Association of Secondary School Principals for making possible youth interviews with state presidents of U.S. student councils. These interviews were set up with the cooperation of Terry Giroux of the National Association of Secondary School Principals.

In addition, gratitude is due Sally Swing Shelley for arranging contacts for the project coordinator with representatives of 17 countries who were assembled for a curriculum conference sponsored by the United Nations late in 1975.

Finally, the writer wishes to pay his respect to persons directly associated with the pleasure and the occasional frustrations of putting together the many component parts of the NEA Project: to Ellen Calabrese and Velma Trussell, the project's executive secretaries who faithfully and skillfully worked on tape transcriptions, text, and general correspondence; to Charles Marshall Plummer for significant help on many facets of the task, including approximately a dozen of the interviews; to David Lee Silvernail for invaluable assistance in translating the project into book form; and last but certainly not least to my wife, Catherine McKenzie Shane, for her professional skill in recording the 95 youth who were interviewed, for perhaps 150 days of "suitcase living" spent on the road during the Bicentennial Year meetings and tapings, and for her love and invariable good humor.

Indiana University
Bloomington, Indiana
October, 1976

Harold G. Shane
Project Coordinator and
University Professor of Education